Sewing  Book

<table>
<tr><td colspan="2" style="background:black;color:white;text-align:center">INFORMATION</td></tr>
</table>

NAME

ADDRESS

E-MAIL ADDRESS

WEBSITE

PHONE   **FAX**

EMERGENCY CONTACT PERSON

PHONE   **FAX**

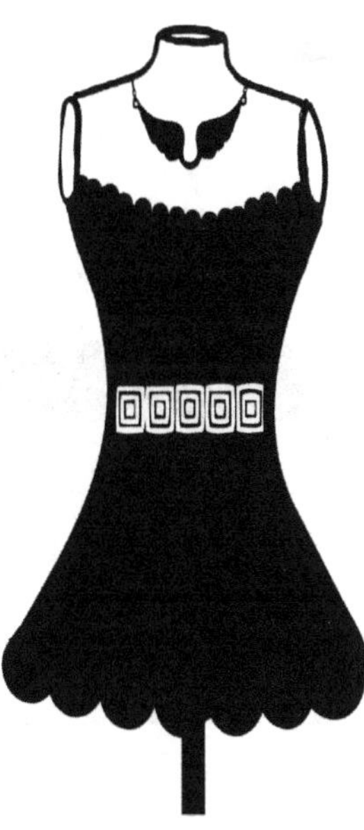

Sewing Log Book

DETAILS

PROJECT ……………………………………………………………

CREATED FOR ……………………………………………………

DATE STARTED …………………… DATE COMPLETED ……………………

ITEM …………………………………………… QTY ……………………

PRICE …………………… DEPOSIT PAID …………… BALANCE PAID ……………

PATTERN USED …………………………………………………………

SUPPLIES NEEDED ………………………………………………………

SKETCH / PHOTO

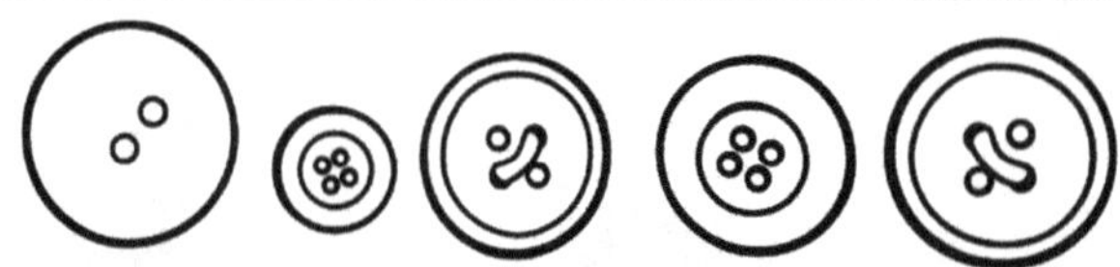

NOTES

…………………………………………………………………………

…………………………………………………………………………

…………………………………………………………………………

…………………………………………………………………………

…………………………………………………………………………

…………………………………………………………………………

Sewing Log Book

DETAILS

PROJECT ....

CREATED FOR ....

DATE STARTED .... DATE COMPLETED ....

ITEM .... QTY ....

PRICE .... DEPOSIT PAID .... BALANCE PAID ....

PATTERN USED ....

SUPPLIES NEEDED ....

SKETCH / PHOTO

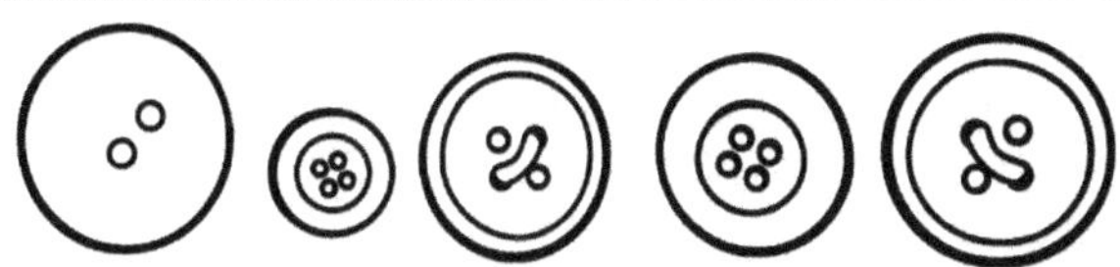

NOTES

....
....
....
....
....
....
....
....

Sewing Log Book

DETAILS

PROJECT ....

CREATED FOR ....

DATE STARTED .... **DATE COMPLETED** ....

ITEM .... **QTY** ....

PRICE .... **DEPOSIT PAID** .... **BALANCE PAID** ....

PATTERN USED ....

SUPPLIES NEEDED ....

SKETCH / PHOTO

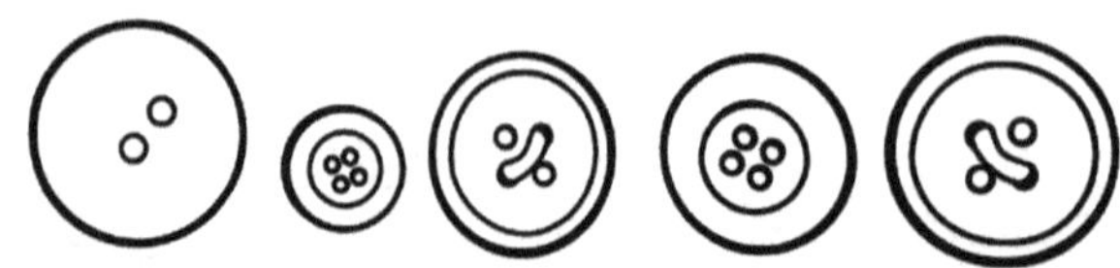

NOTES

....
....
....
....
....
....
....

Sewing Log Book

DETAILS

PROJECT ....

CREATED FOR ....

DATE STARTED .... DATE COMPLETED ....

ITEM .... QTY ....

PRICE .... DEPOSIT PAID .... BALANCE PAID ....

PATTERN USED ....

SUPPLIES NEEDED ....

SKETCH / PHOTO

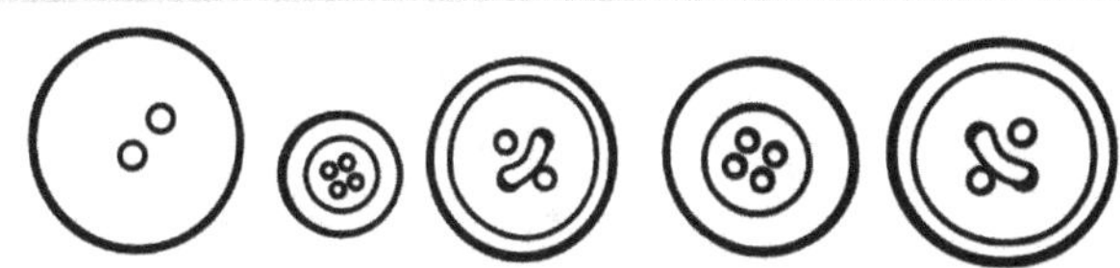

NOTES

....

....

....

....

....

....

....

Sewing Log Book

DETAILS

PROJECT ....

CREATED FOR ....

DATE STARTED .... DATE COMPLETED ....

ITEM .... QTY ....

PRICE .... DEPOSIT PAID .... BALANCE PAID ....

PATTERN USED ....

SUPPLIES NEEDED ....

SKETCH / PHOTO

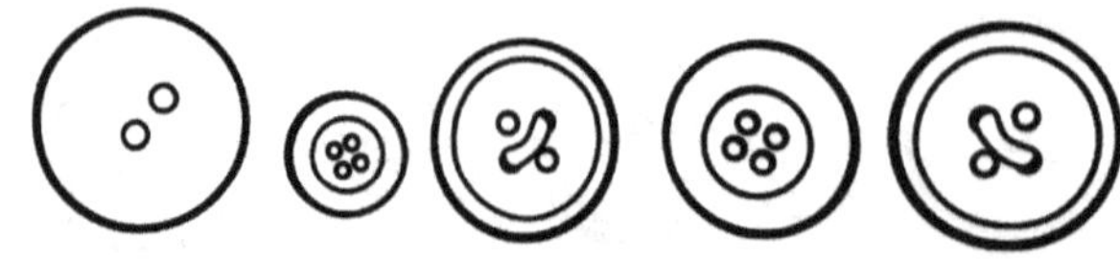

NOTES

....
....
....
....
....
....
....

Sewing Log Book

DETAILS

PROJECT ……………………………………………………………………………

CREATED FOR ………………………………………………………………………

DATE STARTED …………………………… DATE COMPLETED ……………………………

ITEM ………………………………………………… QTY ……………………………

PRICE …………………… DEPOSIT PAID …………… BALANCE PAID ………………

PATTERN USED ………………………………………………………………………

SUPPLIES NEEDED ……………………………………………………………………

SKETCH / PHOTO

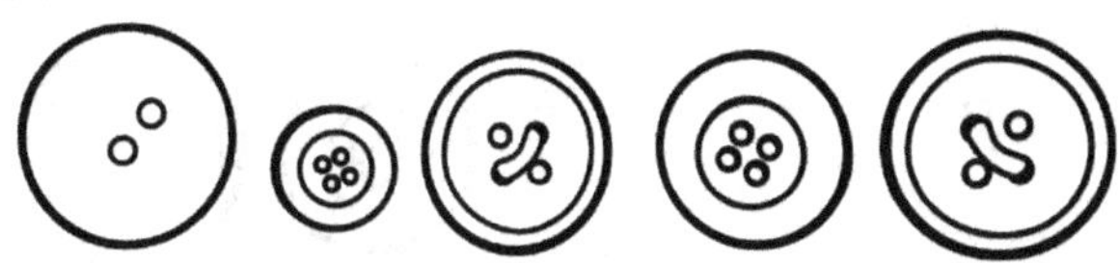

NOTES

……………………………………………………………………………………

……………………………………………………………………………………

……………………………………………………………………………………

……………………………………………………………………………………

……………………………………………………………………………………

……………………………………………………………………………………

……………………………………………………………………………………

Sewing Log Book

DETAILS

PROJECT ....

CREATED FOR ....

DATE STARTED .... DATE COMPLETED ....

ITEM .... QTY ....

PRICE .... DEPOSIT PAID .... BALANCE PAID ....

PATTERN USED ....

SUPPLIES NEEDED ....

SKETCH / PHOTO

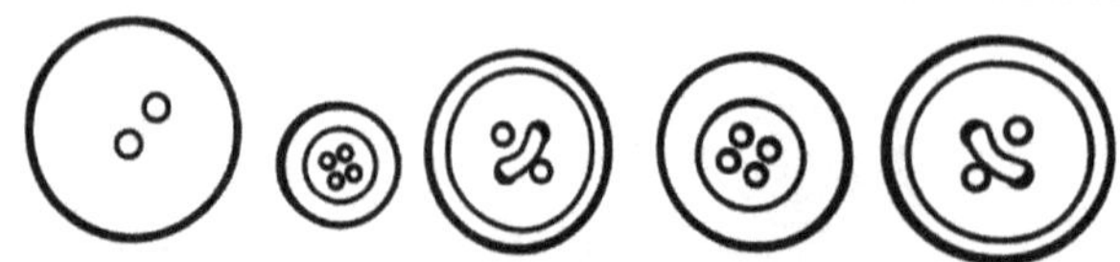

NOTES

....
....
....
....
....
....
....

Sewing Log Book

DETAILS

PROJECT ....

CREATED FOR ....

DATE STARTED .... DATE COMPLETED ....

ITEM .... QTY ....

PRICE .... DEPOSIT PAID .... BALANCE PAID ....

PATTERN USED ....

SUPPLIES NEEDED ....

SKETCH / PHOTO

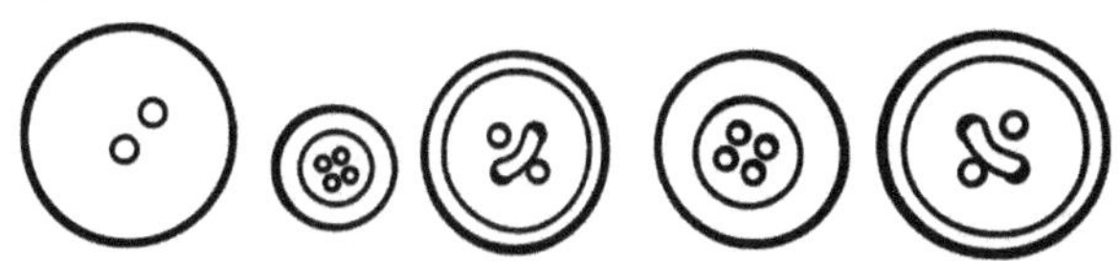

NOTES

....
....
....
....
....
....
....
....

Sewing Log Book

DETAILS

PROJECT ....

CREATED FOR ....

DATE STARTED .... DATE COMPLETED ....

ITEM .... QTY ....

PRICE .... DEPOSIT PAID .... BALANCE PAID ....

PATTERN USED ....

SUPPLIES NEEDED ....

SKETCH / PHOTO

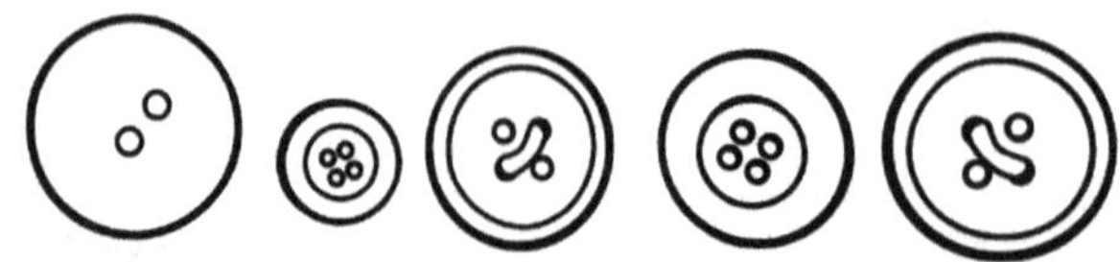

NOTES

....

....

....

....

....

....

....

Sewing Log Book

DETAILS

PROJECT ....

CREATED FOR ....

DATE STARTED .... DATE COMPLETED ....

ITEM .... QTY ....

PRICE .... DEPOSIT PAID .... BALANCE PAID ....

PATTERN USED ....

SUPPLIES NEEDED ....

SKETCH / PHOTO

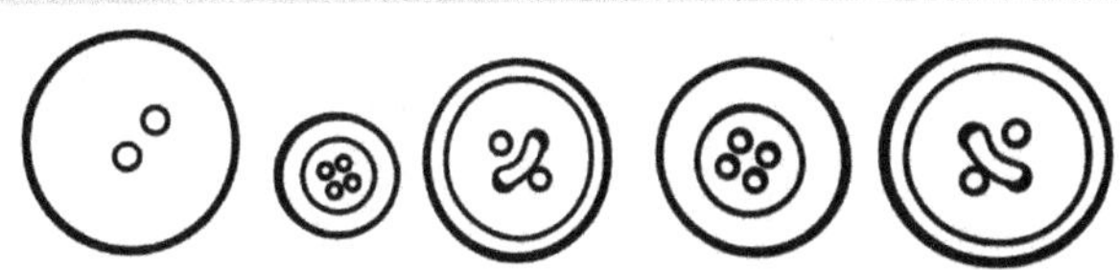

NOTES

....

....

....

....

....

....

....

Sewing Log Book

DETAILS

PROJECT ....

CREATED FOR ....

DATE STARTED .... DATE COMPLETED ....

ITEM .... QTY ....

PRICE .... DEPOSIT PAID .... BALANCE PAID ....

PATTERN USED ....

SUPPLIES NEEDED ....

SKETCH / PHOTO

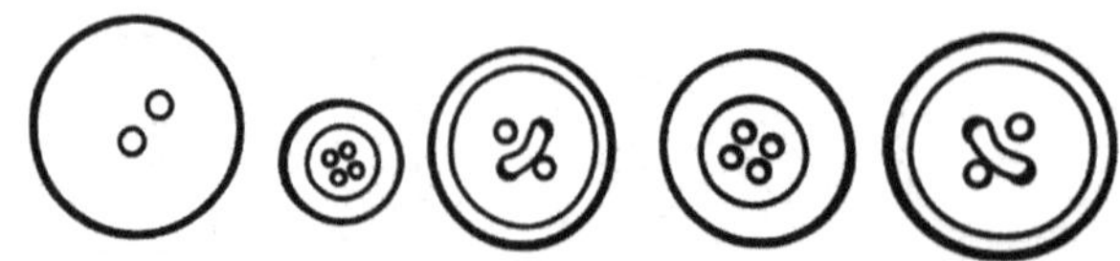

NOTES

....

....

....

....

....

....

....

Sewing Log Book

PROJECT ....

CREATED FOR ....

DATE STARTED .... DATE COMPLETED ....

ITEM .... QTY ....

PRICE .... DEPOSIT PAID .... BALANCE PAID ....

PATTERN USED ....

SUPPLIES NEEDED ....

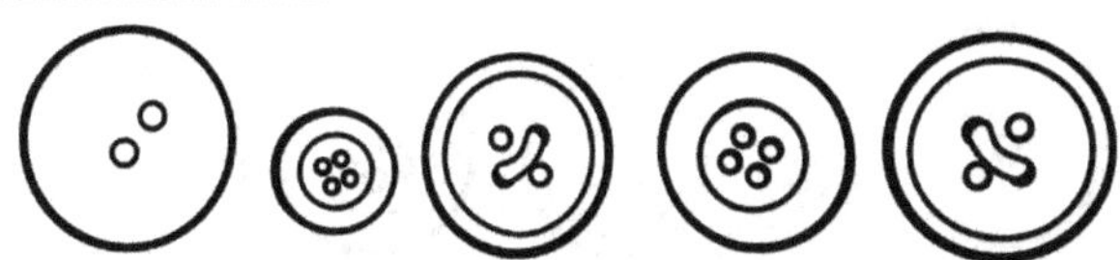

....

....

....

....

....

....

....

Sewing Log Book

DETAILS

PROJECT ....

CREATED FOR ....

DATE STARTED .... DATE COMPLETED ....

ITEM .... QTY ....

PRICE .... DEPOSIT PAID .... BALANCE PAID ....

PATTERN USED ....

SUPPLIES NEEDED ....

SKETCH / PHOTO

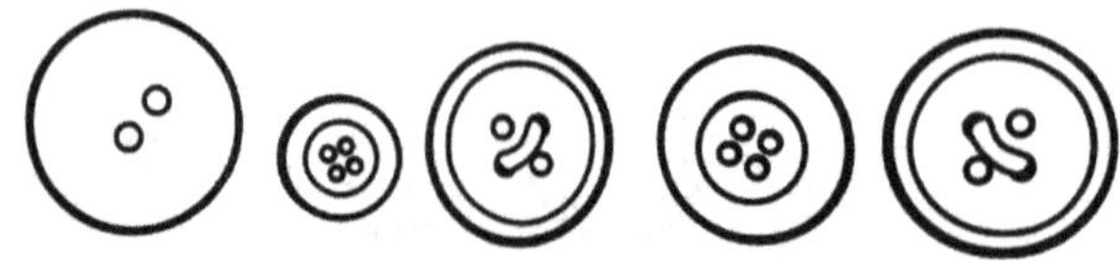

NOTES

....
....
....
....
....
....
....

Sewing Log Book

DETAILS

PROJECT ....

CREATED FOR ....

DATE STARTED .... DATE COMPLETED ....

ITEM .... QTY ....

PRICE .... DEPOSIT PAID .... BALANCE PAID ......

PATTERN USED ....

SUPPLIES NEEDED ....

SKETCH / PHOTO

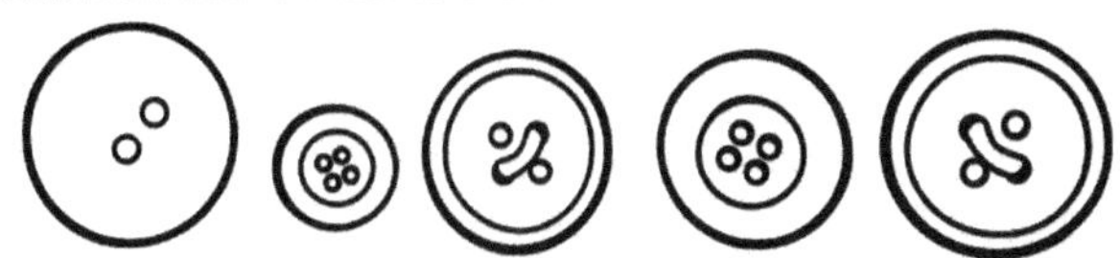

NOTES

....
....
....
....
....
....
....

Sewing Log Book

DETAILS

PROJECT ....

CREATED FOR ....

DATE STARTED .... DATE COMPLETED ....

ITEM .... QTY ....

PRICE .... DEPOSIT PAID .... BALANCE PAID ....

PATTERN USED ....

SUPPLIES NEEDED ....

SKETCH / PHOTO

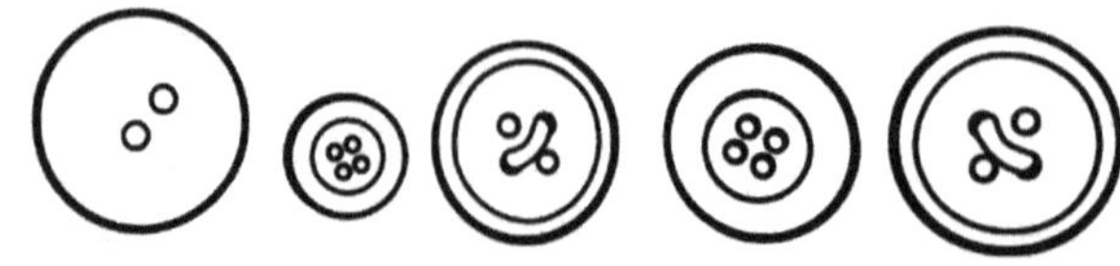

NOTES

....

....

....

....

....

....

Sewing Log Book

DETAILS

PROJECT ....

CREATED FOR ....

DATE STARTED .... **DATE COMPLETED** ....

ITEM .... **QTY** ....

PRICE .... **DEPOSIT PAID** .... **BALANCE PAID** ....

PATTERN USED ....

SUPPLIES NEEDED ....

SKETCH / PHOTO

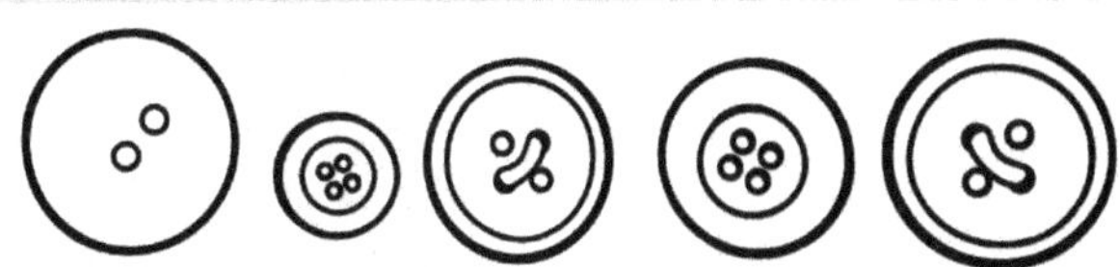

NOTES

....
....
....
....
....
....
....

Sewing Log Book

DETAILS

PROJECT ....

CREATED FOR ....

DATE STARTED .... **DATE COMPLETED** ....

ITEM .... **QTY** ....

PRICE .... **DEPOSIT PAID** .... **BALANCE PAID** ....

PATTERN USED ....

SUPPLIES NEEDED ....

SKETCH / PHOTO

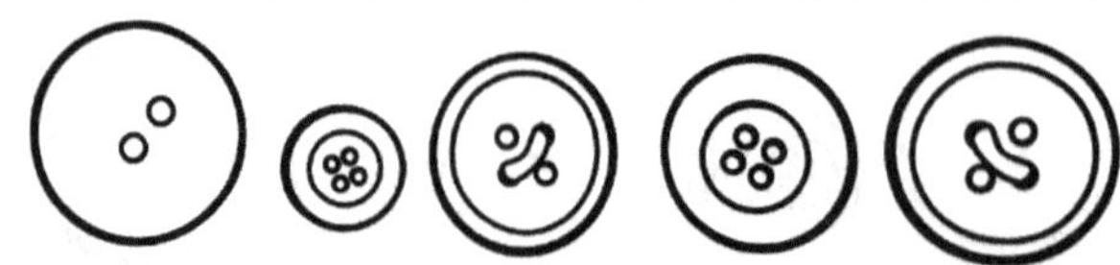

NOTES

....
....
....
....
....
....
....

Sewing Log Book

DETAILS

PROJECT ....

CREATED FOR ....

DATE STARTED .... **DATE COMPLETED** ....

ITEM .... **QTY** ....

PRICE .... **DEPOSIT PAID** .... **BALANCE PAID** ....

PATTERN USED ....

SUPPLIES NEEDED ....

SKETCH / PHOTO

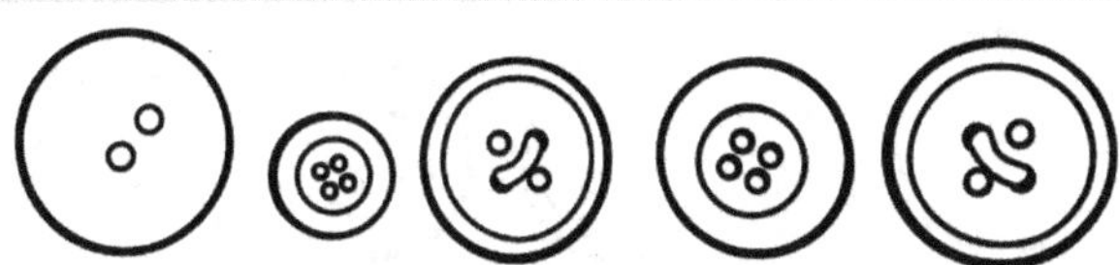

NOTES

....
....
....
....
....
....
....
....

Sewing Log Book

DETAILS

PROJECT ....

CREATED FOR ....

DATE STARTED .... DATE COMPLETED ....

ITEM .... QTY ....

PRICE .... DEPOSIT PAID .... BALANCE PAID ....

PATTERN USED ....

SUPPLIES NEEDED ....

SKETCH / PHOTO

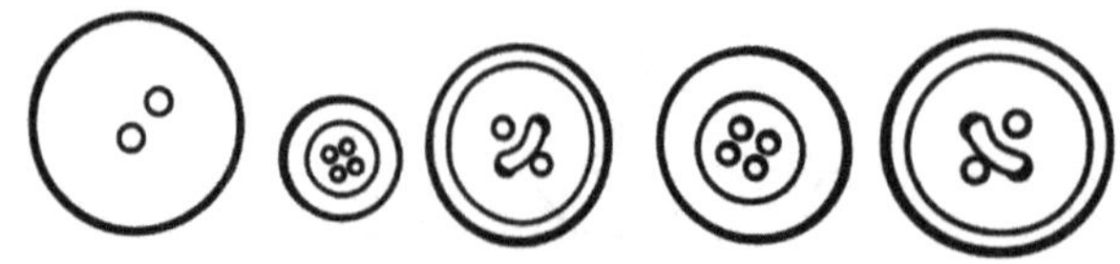

NOTES

....
....
....
....
....
....
....

Sewing Log Book

DETAILS

PROJECT ....

CREATED FOR ....

DATE STARTED .... DATE COMPLETED ....

ITEM .... QTY ....

PRICE .... DEPOSIT PAID .... BALANCE PAID ....

PATTERN USED ....

SUPPLIES NEEDED ....

SKETCH / PHOTO

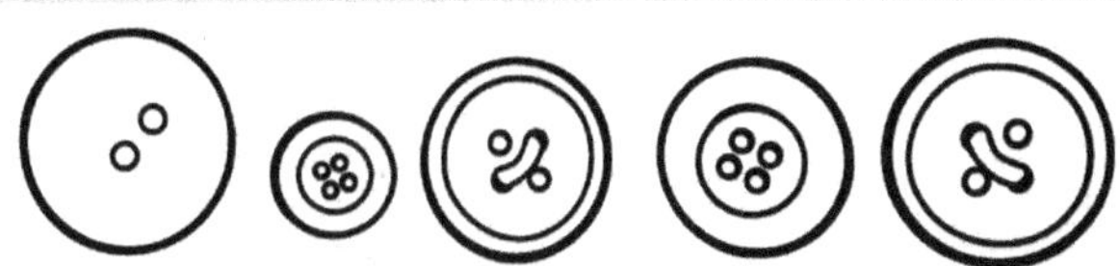

NOTES

....
....
....
....
....
....
....
....

Sewing Log Book

DETAILS

PROJECT ....

CREATED FOR ....

DATE STARTED .... DATE COMPLETED ....

ITEM .... QTY ....

PRICE .... DEPOSIT PAID .... BALANCE PAID ....

PATTERN USED ....

SUPPLIES NEEDED ....

SKETCH / PHOTO

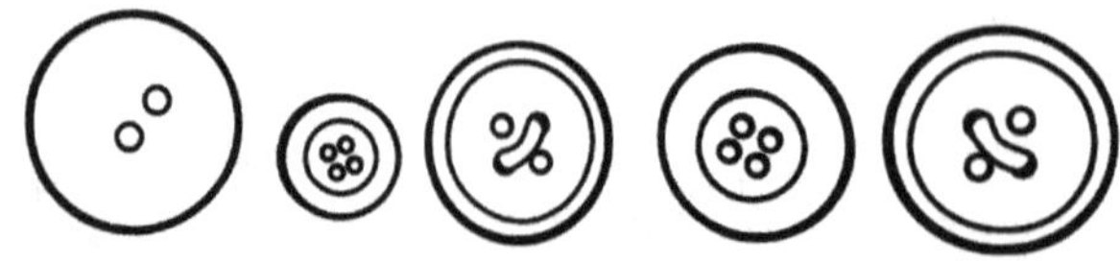

NOTES

....

....

....

....

....

....

....

Sewing Log Book

DETAILS

PROJECT ....

CREATED FOR ....

DATE STARTED .... DATE COMPLETED ....

ITEM .... QTY ....

PRICE .... DEPOSIT PAID .... BALANCE PAID ....

PATTERN USED ....

SUPPLIES NEEDED ....

SKETCH / PHOTO

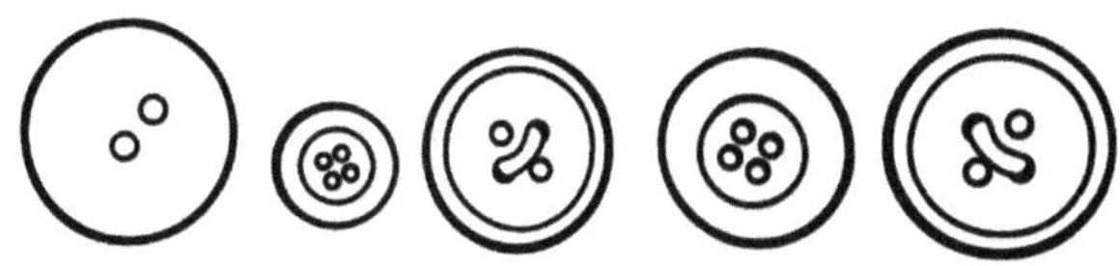

NOTES

....

....

....

....

....

....

Sewing Log Book

PROJECT ....

CREATED FOR ....

DATE STARTED .... **DATE COMPLETED** ....

ITEM .... **QTY** ....

PRICE .... **DEPOSIT PAID** .... **BALANCE PAID** ....

PATTERN USED ....

SUPPLIES NEEDED ....

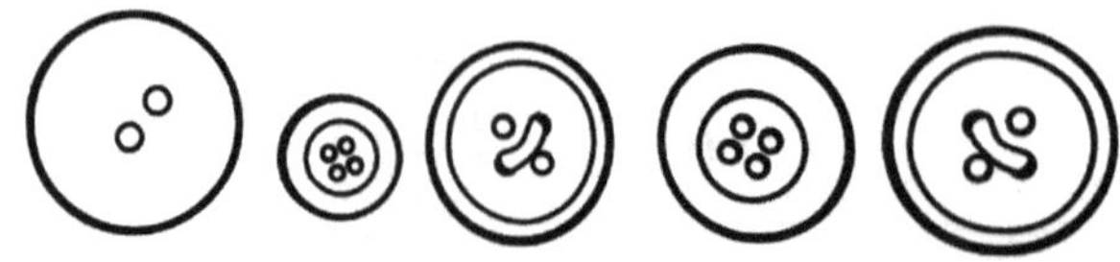

....
....
....
....
....
....
....

Sewing Log Book

PROJECT ....

CREATED FOR ....

DATE STARTED .... **DATE COMPLETED** ....

ITEM .... **QTY** ....

PRICE .... **DEPOSIT PAID** .... **BALANCE PAID** ....

PATTERN USED ....

SUPPLIES NEEDED ....

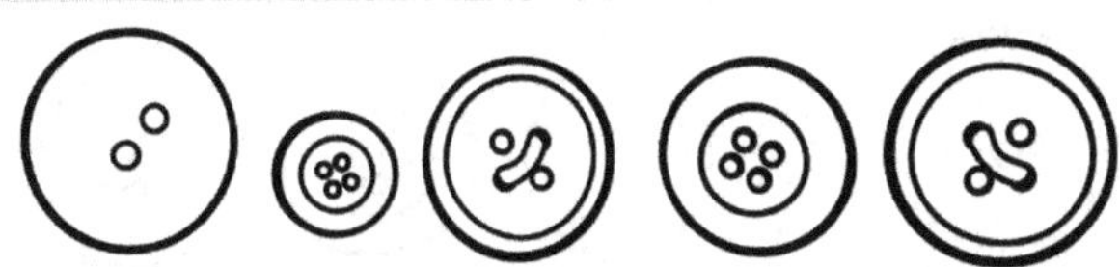

....
....
....
....
....
....
....

Sewing Log Book

DETAILS

PROJECT ....

CREATED FOR ....

DATE STARTED .... DATE COMPLETED ....

ITEM .... QTY ....

PRICE .... DEPOSIT PAID .... BALANCE PAID ....

PATTERN USED ....

SUPPLIES NEEDED ....

SKETCH / PHOTO

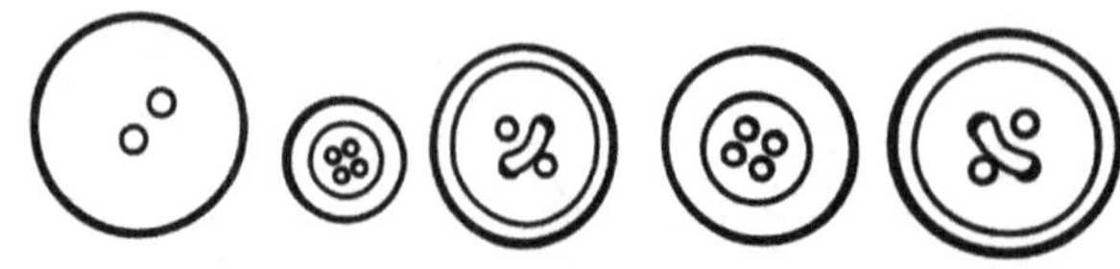

NOTES

....
....
....
....
....
....
....

Sewing Log Book

DETAILS

PROJECT ....

CREATED FOR ....

DATE STARTED .... DATE COMPLETED ....

ITEM .... QTY ....

PRICE .... DEPOSIT PAID .... BALANCE PAID ....

PATTERN USED ....

SUPPLIES NEEDED ....

SKETCH / PHOTO

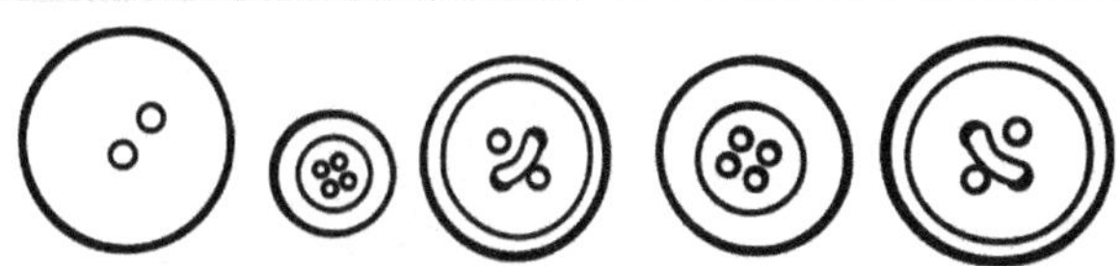

NOTES

....
....
....
....
....
....
....

Sewing Log Book

PROJECT ....

CREATED FOR ....

DATE STARTED .... DATE COMPLETED ....

ITEM .... QTY ....

PRICE .... DEPOSIT PAID .... BALANCE PAID ....

PATTERN USED ....

SUPPLIES NEEDED ....

SKETCH / PHOTO

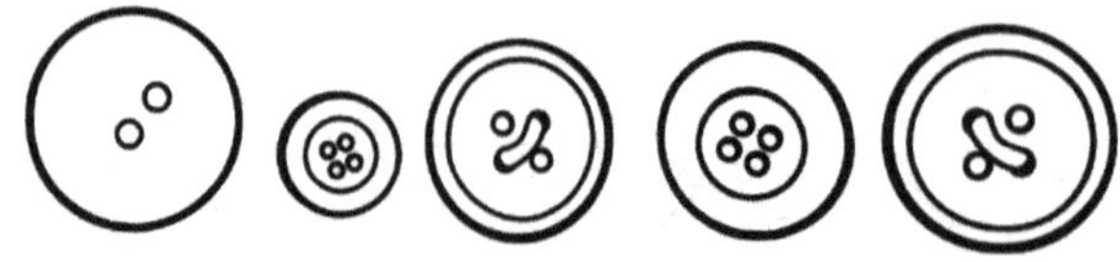

NOTES

....

....

....

....

....

....

....

Sewing Log Book

DETAILS

PROJECT ....

CREATED FOR ....

DATE STARTED .... DATE COMPLETED ....

ITEM .... QTY ....

PRICE .... DEPOSIT PAID .... BALANCE PAID ....

PATTERN USED ....

SUPPLIES NEEDED ....

SKETCH / PHOTO

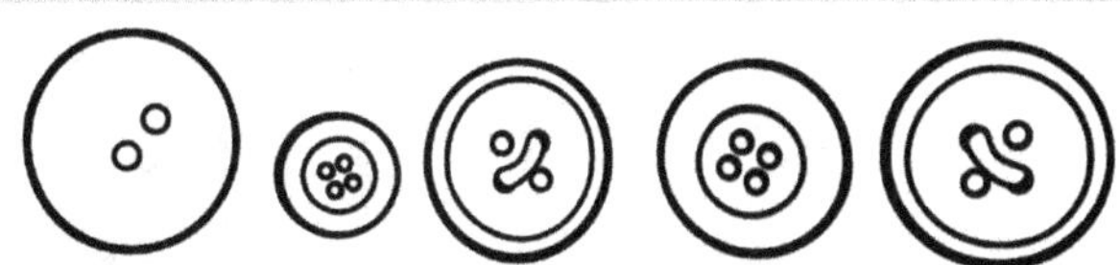

NOTES

....
....
....
....
....
....
....

Sewing Log Book

DETAILS

PROJECT ....

CREATED FOR ....

DATE STARTED .... DATE COMPLETED ....

ITEM .... QTY ....

PRICE .... DEPOSIT PAID .... BALANCE PAID ....

PATTERN USED ....

SUPPLIES NEEDED ....

SKETCH / PHOTO

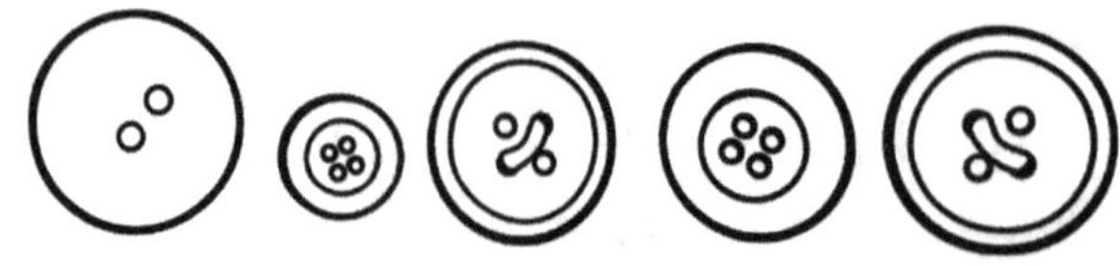

NOTES

....

....

....

....

....

....

....

Sewing Log Book

DETAILS

PROJECT ....

CREATED FOR ....

DATE STARTED .... **DATE COMPLETED** ....

ITEM .... **QTY** ....

PRICE .... **DEPOSIT PAID** .... **BALANCE PAID** ....

PATTERN USED ....

SUPPLIES NEEDED ....

SKETCH / PHOTO

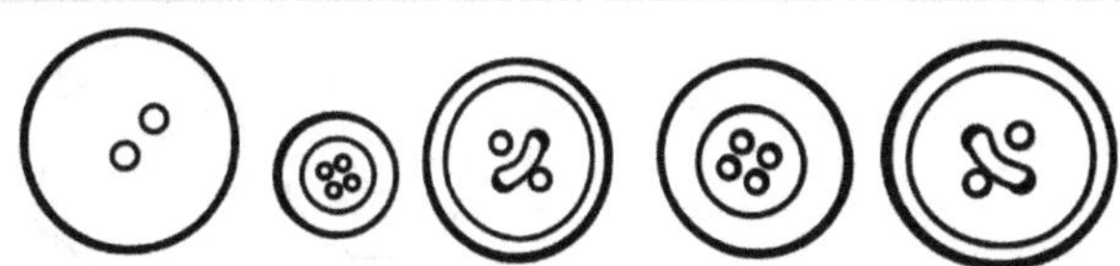

NOTES

....

....

....

....

....

....

....

Sewing Log Book

DETAILS

PROJECT ....

CREATED FOR ....

DATE STARTED .... DATE COMPLETED ....

ITEM .... QTY ....

PRICE .... DEPOSIT PAID .... BALANCE PAID ....

PATTERN USED ....

SUPPLIES NEEDED ....

SKETCH / PHOTO

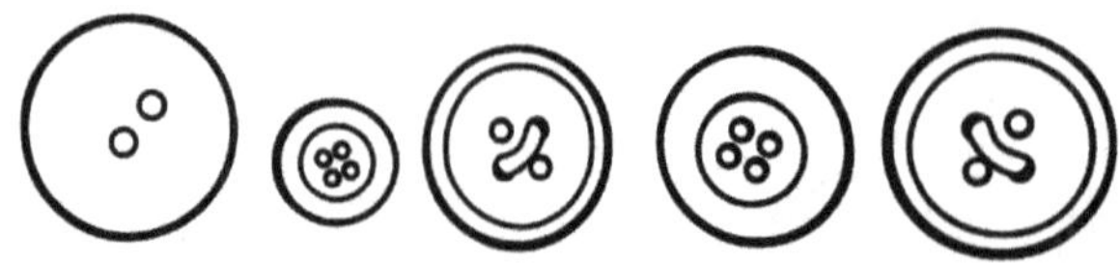

NOTES

....

....

....

....

....

....

....

Sewing Log Book

DETAILS

PROJECT ....

CREATED FOR ....

DATE STARTED .... DATE COMPLETED ....

ITEM .... QTY ....

PRICE .... DEPOSIT PAID .... BALANCE PAID ....

PATTERN USED ....

SUPPLIES NEEDED ....

SKETCH / PHOTO

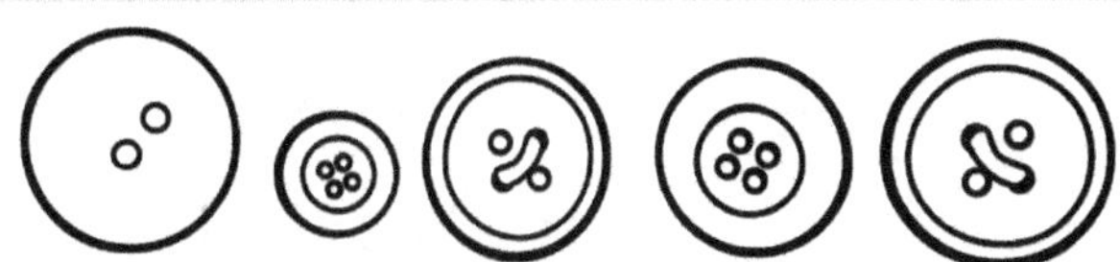

NOTES

....
....
....
....
....
....
....

Sewing Log Book

DETAILS

PROJECT ....

CREATED FOR ....

DATE STARTED .... DATE COMPLETED ....

ITEM .... QTY ....

PRICE .... DEPOSIT PAID .... BALANCE PAID ....

PATTERN USED ....

SUPPLIES NEEDED ....

SKETCH / PHOTO

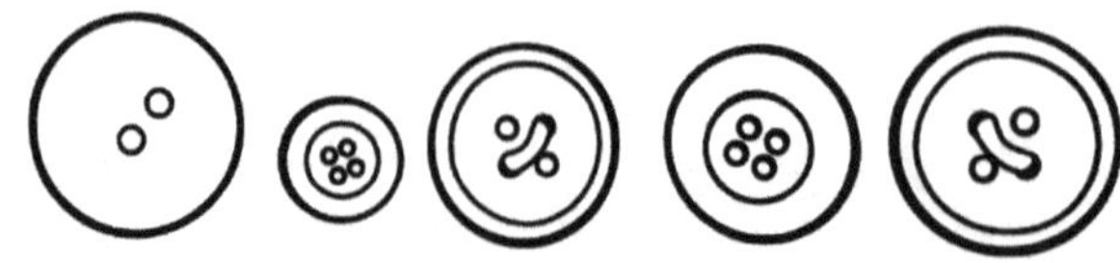

NOTES

....

....

....

....

....

....

....

Sewing Log Book

DETAILS

PROJECT ....

CREATED FOR ....

DATE STARTED .... DATE COMPLETED ....

ITEM .... QTY ....

PRICE .... DEPOSIT PAID .... BALANCE PAID ....

PATTERN USED ....

SUPPLIES NEEDED ....

SKETCH / PHOTO

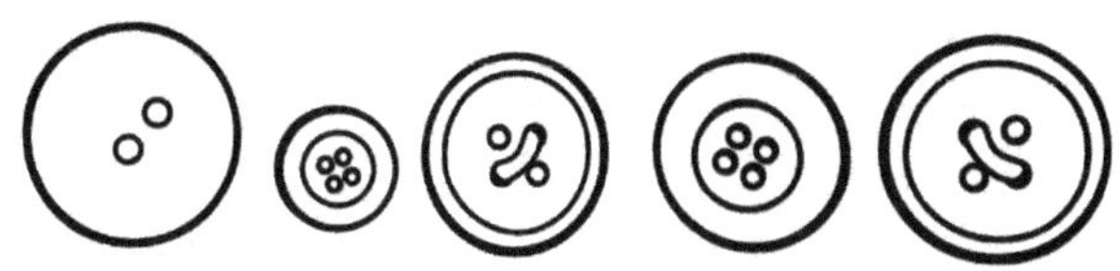

NOTES

....

....

....

....

....

....

....

Sewing Log Book

DETAILS

PROJECT ....

CREATED FOR ....

DATE STARTED .... DATE COMPLETED ....

ITEM .... QTY ....

PRICE .... DEPOSIT PAID .... BALANCE PAID ....

PATTERN USED ....

SUPPLIES NEEDED ....

SKETCH / PHOTO

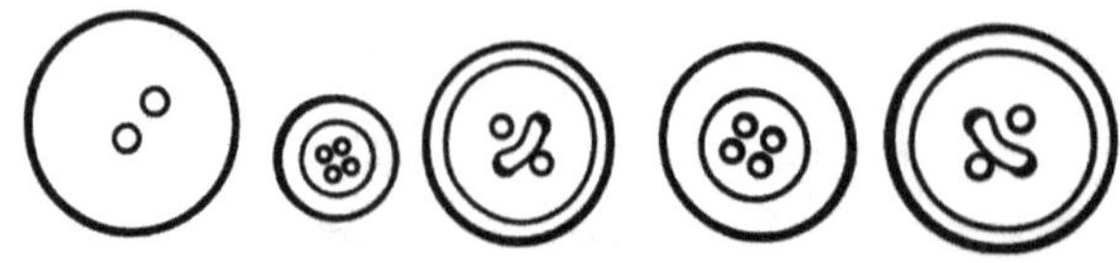

NOTES

....
....
....
....
....
....

Sewing Log Book

DETAILS

PROJECT ....

CREATED FOR ....

DATE STARTED .... DATE COMPLETED ....

ITEM .... QTY ....

PRICE .... DEPOSIT PAID .... BALANCE PAID ....

PATTERN USED ....

SUPPLIES NEEDED ....

SKETCH / PHOTO

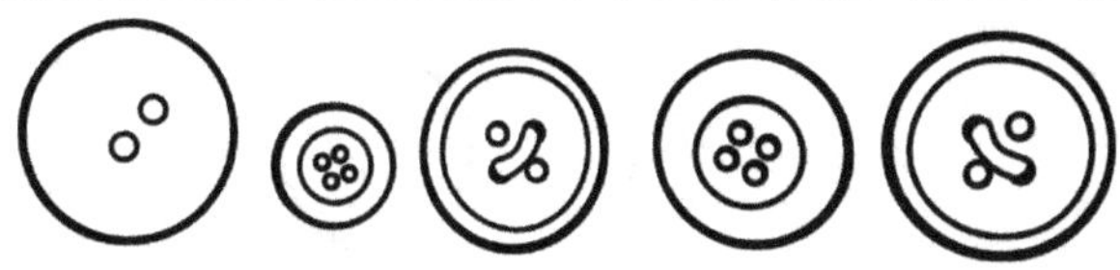

NOTES

....
....
....
....
....
....
....

Sewing Log Book

DETAILS

PROJECT ....

CREATED FOR ....

DATE STARTED .... DATE COMPLETED ....

ITEM .... QTY ....

PRICE .... DEPOSIT PAID .... BALANCE PAID ....

PATTERN USED ....

SUPPLIES NEEDED ....

SKETCH / PHOTO

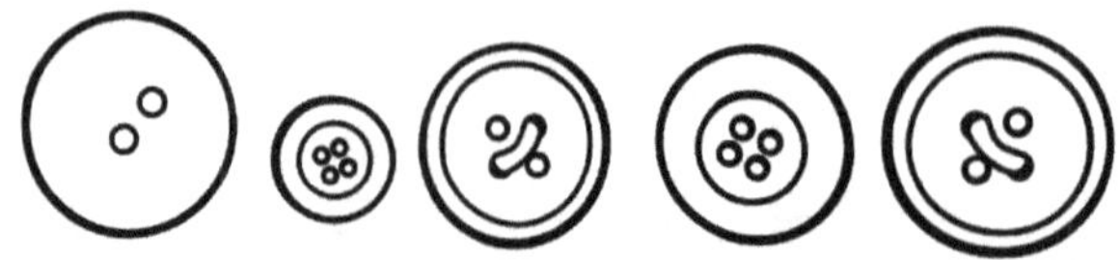

NOTES

....
....
....
....
....
....
....

Sewing Log Book

PROJECT ....

CREATED FOR ....

DATE STARTED .... DATE COMPLETED ....

ITEM .... QTY ....

PRICE .... DEPOSIT PAID .... BALANCE PAID ....

PATTERN USED ....

SUPPLIES NEEDED ....

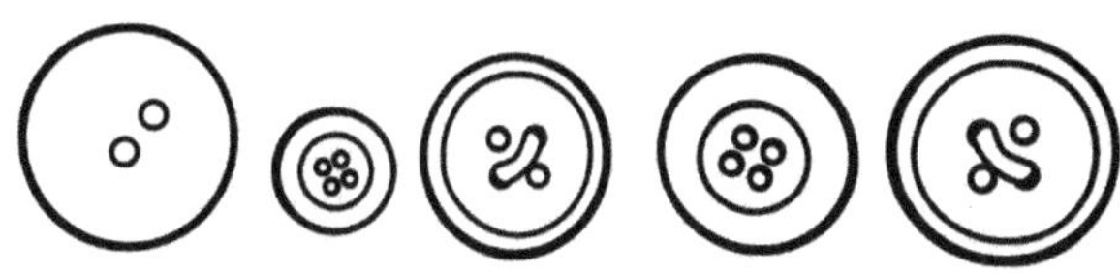

....
....
....
....
....
....
....

Sewing Log Book

DETAILS

PROJECT …………………………………………………………………………

CREATED FOR …………………………………………………………………

DATE STARTED ………………………… DATE COMPLETED ……………………

ITEM ……………………………………… QTY ……………………

PRICE ………………… DEPOSIT PAID ………………… BALANCE PAID …………………

PATTERN USED …………………………………………………………………

SUPPLIES NEEDED ………………………………………………………………

SKETCH / PHOTO

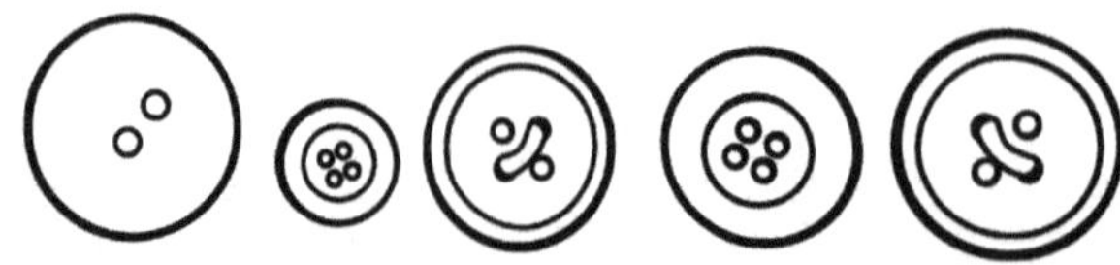

NOTES

…………………………………………………………………………………
…………………………………………………………………………………
…………………………………………………………………………………
…………………………………………………………………………………
…………………………………………………………………………………
…………………………………………………………………………………
…………………………………………………………………………………

Sewing Log Book

DETAILS

PROJECT ....

CREATED FOR ....

DATE STARTED .... **DATE COMPLETED** ....

ITEM .... **QTY** ....

PRICE .... **DEPOSIT PAID** .... **BALANCE PAID** ....

PATTERN USED ....

SUPPLIES NEEDED ....

SKETCH / PHOTO

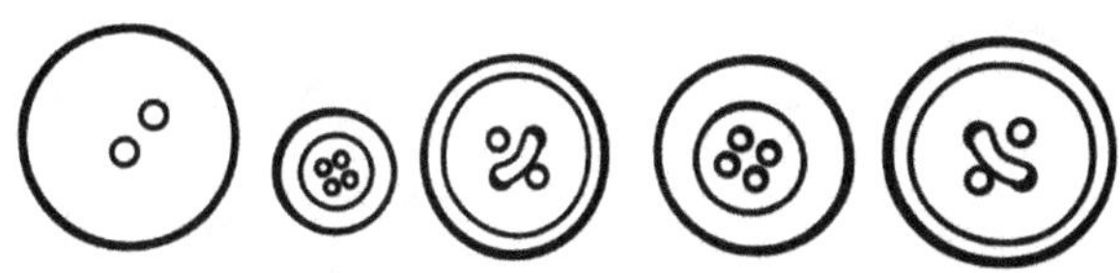

NOTES

....
....
....
....
....
....
....

Sewing Log Book

DETAILS

PROJECT ....

CREATED FOR ....

DATE STARTED .... DATE COMPLETED ....

ITEM .... QTY ....

PRICE .... DEPOSIT PAID .... BALANCE PAID ....

PATTERN USED ....

SUPPLIES NEEDED ....

SKETCH / PHOTO

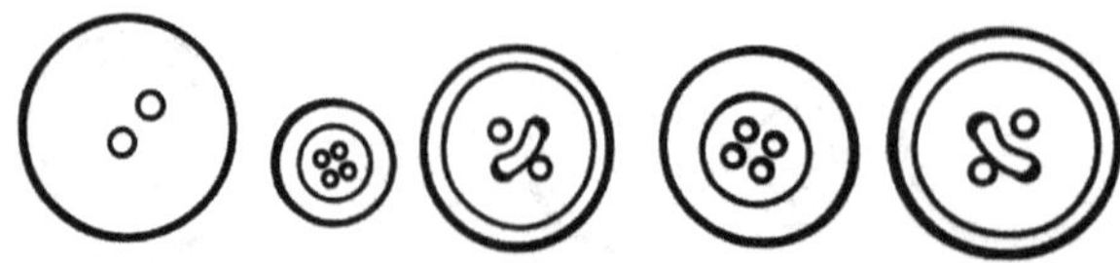

NOTES

....
....
....
....
....
....
....

Sewing Log Book

DETAILS

PROJECT ....

CREATED FOR ....

DATE STARTED .... DATE COMPLETED ....

ITEM .... QTY ....

PRICE .... DEPOSIT PAID .... BALANCE PAID ....

PATTERN USED ....

SUPPLIES NEEDED ....

SKETCH / PHOTO

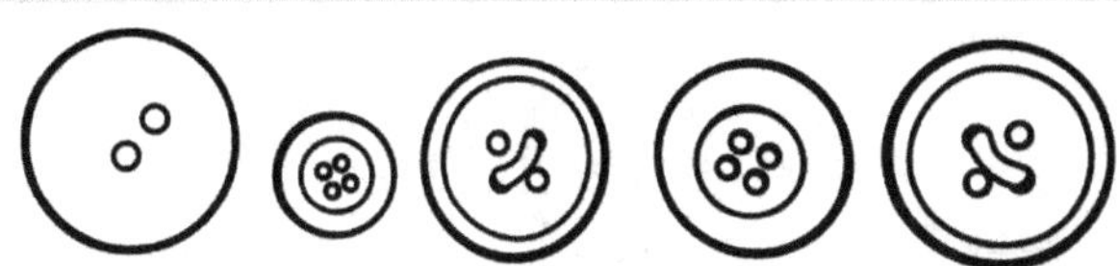

NOTES

....

....

....

....

....

....

....

Sewing Log Book

DETAILS

PROJECT ....

CREATED FOR ....

DATE STARTED .... DATE COMPLETED ....

ITEM .... QTY ....

PRICE .... DEPOSIT PAID .... BALANCE PAID ....

PATTERN USED ....

SUPPLIES NEEDED ....

SKETCH / PHOTO

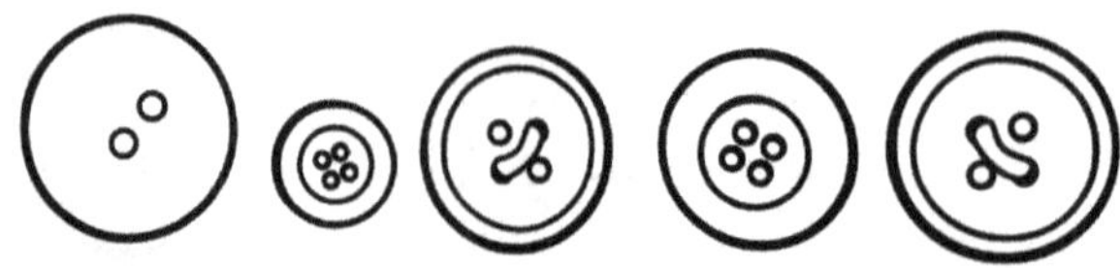

NOTES

....
....
....
....
....
....

Sewing Log Book

DETAILS

PROJECT ....

CREATED FOR ....

DATE STARTED .... DATE COMPLETED ....

ITEM .... QTY ....

PRICE .... DEPOSIT PAID .... BALANCE PAID ....

PATTERN USED ....

SUPPLIES NEEDED ....

SKETCH / PHOTO

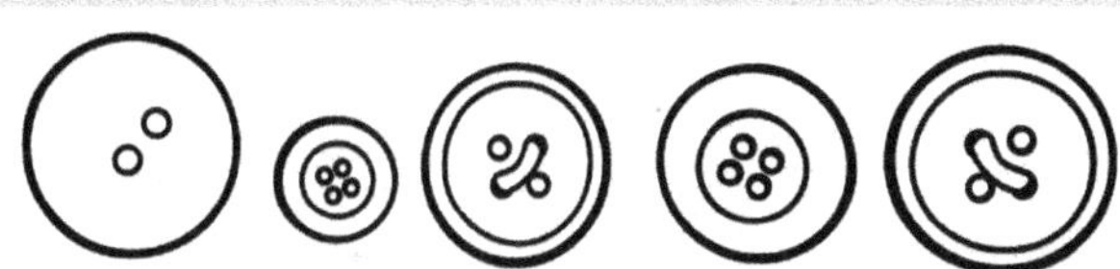

NOTES

....
....
....
....
....
....
....

Sewing Log Book

DETAILS

PROJECT ....

CREATED FOR ....

DATE STARTED .... DATE COMPLETED ....

ITEM .... QTY ....

PRICE .... DEPOSIT PAID .... BALANCE PAID ....

PATTERN USED ....

SUPPLIES NEEDED ....

SKETCH / PHOTO

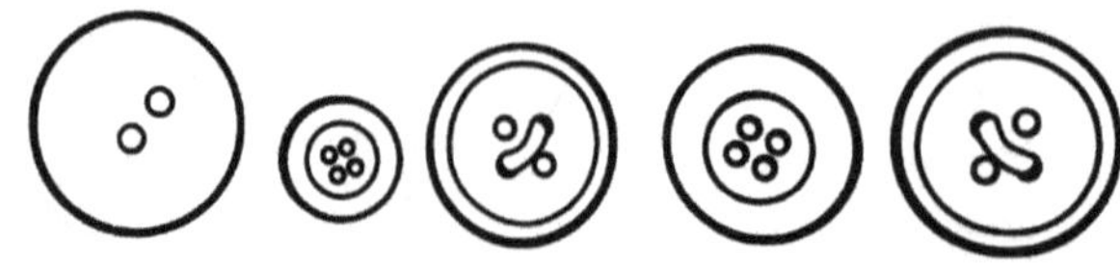

NOTES

....
....
....
....
....
....
....

Sewing Log Book

DETAILS

PROJECT ....

CREATED FOR ....

DATE STARTED .... **DATE COMPLETED** ....

ITEM .... **QTY** ....

PRICE .... **DEPOSIT PAID** .... **BALANCE PAID** ....

PATTERN USED ....

SUPPLIES NEEDED ....

SKETCH / PHOTO

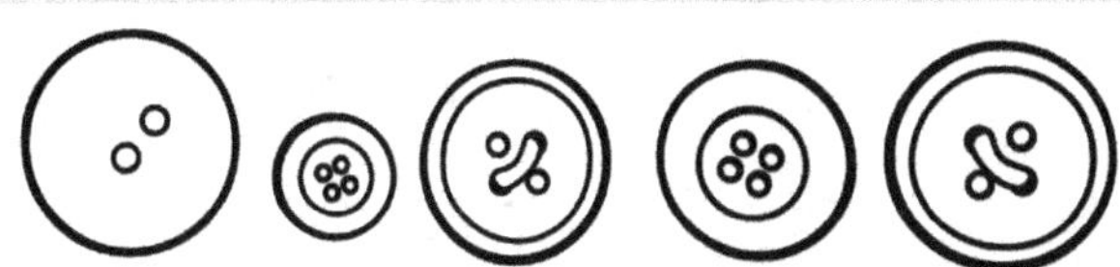

NOTES

....
....
....
....
....
....
....
....

Sewing Log Book

DETAILS

PROJECT ....

CREATED FOR ....

DATE STARTED .... **DATE COMPLETED** ....

ITEM .... **QTY** ....

PRICE .... **DEPOSIT PAID** .... **BALANCE PAID** ....

PATTERN USED ....

SUPPLIES NEEDED ....

SKETCH / PHOTO

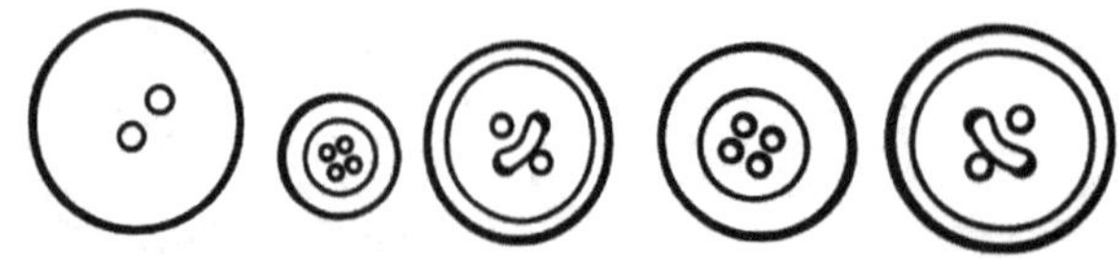

NOTES

....

....

....

....

....

....

....

Sewing Log Book

PROJECT ....

CREATED FOR ....

DATE STARTED .... **DATE COMPLETED** ....

ITEM .... **QTY** ....

PRICE .... **DEPOSIT PAID** .... **BALANCE PAID** ....

PATTERN USED ....

SUPPLIES NEEDED ....

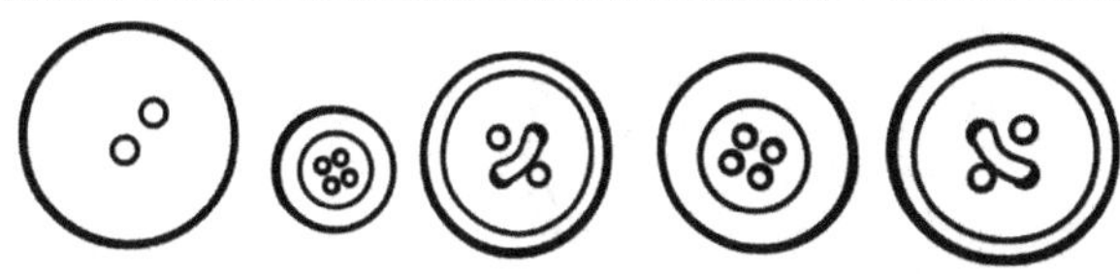

....
....
....
....
....
....
....

Sewing Log Book

DETAILS

PROJECT ....

CREATED FOR ....

DATE STARTED .... DATE COMPLETED ....

ITEM .... QTY ....

PRICE .... DEPOSIT PAID .... BALANCE PAID ....

PATTERN USED ....

SUPPLIES NEEDED ....

SKETCH / PHOTO

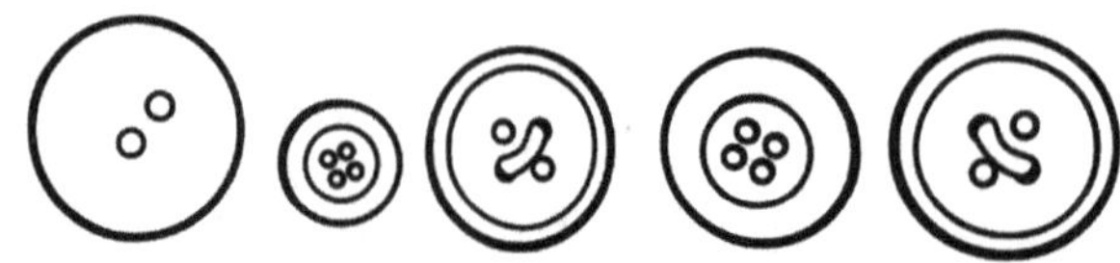

NOTES

....

....

....

....

....

....

....

Sewing Log Book

DETAILS

PROJECT ....

CREATED FOR ....

DATE STARTED .... DATE COMPLETED ....

ITEM .... QTY ....

PRICE .... DEPOSIT PAID .... BALANCE PAID ....

PATTERN USED ....

SUPPLIES NEEDED ....

SKETCH / PHOTO

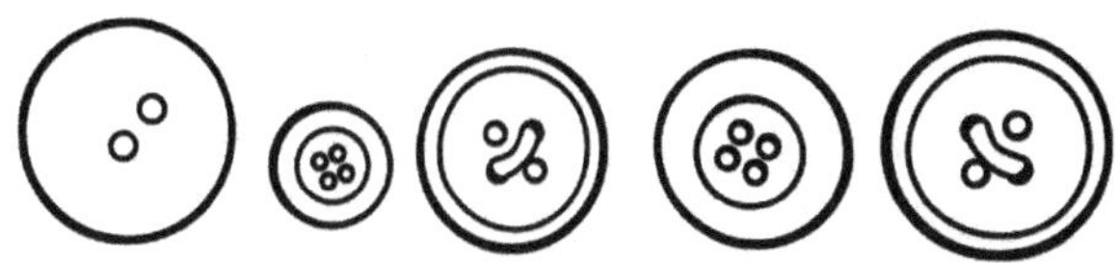

NOTES

....

....

....

....

....

....

....

Sewing Log Book

PROJECT ....

CREATED FOR ....

DATE STARTED .... DATE COMPLETED ....

ITEM .... QTY ....

PRICE .... DEPOSIT PAID .... BALANCE PAID ....

PATTERN USED ....

SUPPLIES NEEDED ....

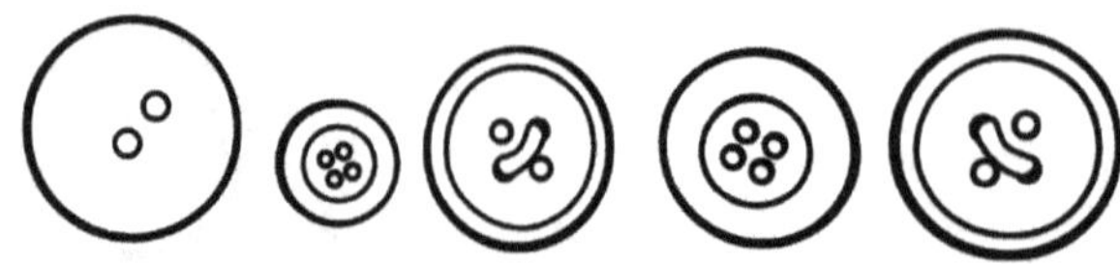

....
....
....
....
....
....
....
....

Sewing Log Book

DETAILS

PROJECT ....

CREATED FOR ....

DATE STARTED .... DATE COMPLETED ....

ITEM .... QTY ....

PRICE .... DEPOSIT PAID .... BALANCE PAID ....

PATTERN USED ....

SUPPLIES NEEDED ....

SKETCH / PHOTO

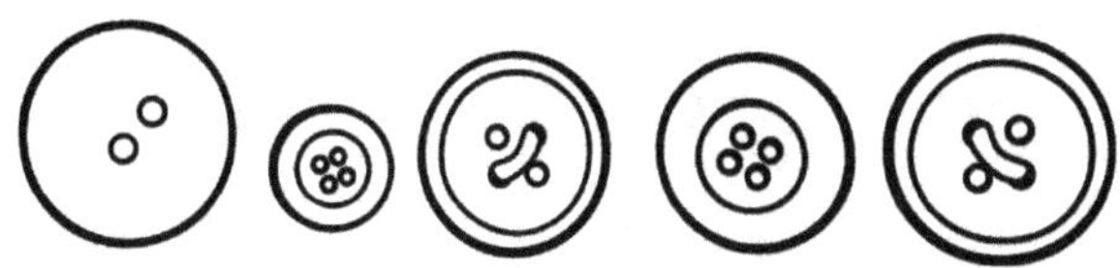

NOTES

....
....
....
....
....
....
....

Sewing Log Book

PROJECT ....

CREATED FOR ....

DATE STARTED .... **DATE COMPLETED** ....

ITEM .... **QTY** ....

PRICE .... **DEPOSIT PAID** .... **BALANCE PAID** ....

PATTERN USED ....

SUPPLIES NEEDED ....

SKETCH / PHOTO

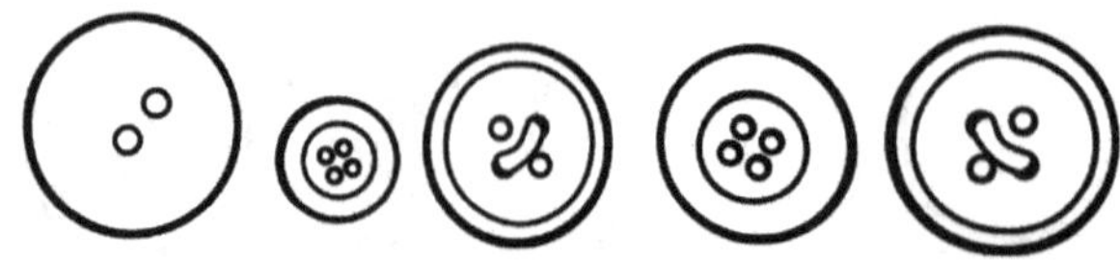

NOTES

....

....

....

....

....

....

....

Sewing Log Book

PROJECT ....

CREATED FOR ....

DATE STARTED .... DATE COMPLETED ....

ITEM .... QTY ....

PRICE .... DEPOSIT PAID .... BALANCE PAID ....

PATTERN USED ....

SUPPLIES NEEDED ....

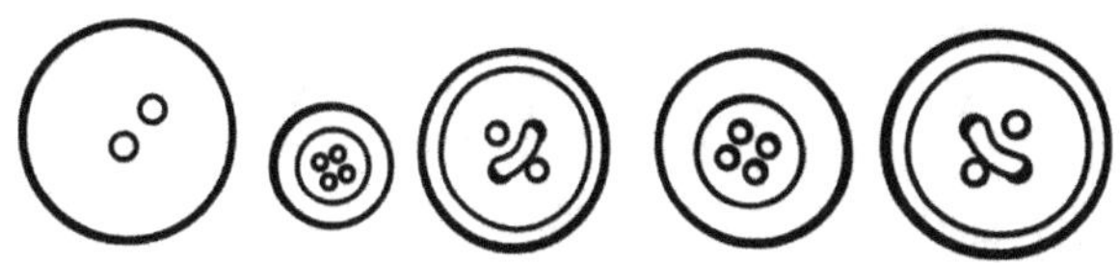

....
....
....
....
....
....
....

Sewing Log Book

DETAILS

PROJECT ....

CREATED FOR ....

DATE STARTED .... DATE COMPLETED ....

ITEM .... QTY ....

PRICE .... DEPOSIT PAID .... BALANCE PAID ....

PATTERN USED ....

SUPPLIES NEEDED ....

SKETCH / PHOTO

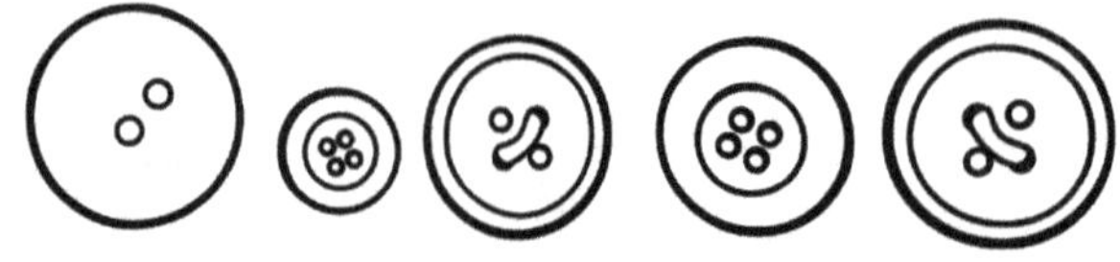

NOTES

....
....
....
....
....
....
....

Sewing Log Book

DETAILS

PROJECT ....

CREATED FOR ....

DATE STARTED .... **DATE COMPLETED** ....

ITEM .... **QTY** ....

PRICE .... **DEPOSIT PAID** .... **BALANCE PAID** ....

PATTERN USED ....

SUPPLIES NEEDED ....

SKETCH / PHOTO

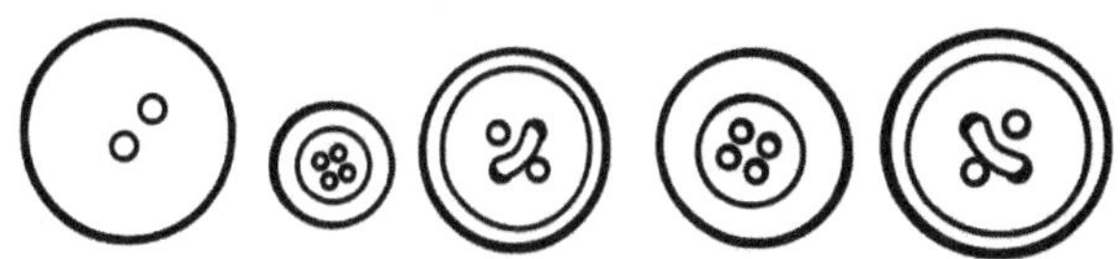

NOTES

....
....
....
....
....
....
....

Sewing Log Book

DETAILS

PROJECT ....

CREATED FOR ....

DATE STARTED .... DATE COMPLETED ....

ITEM .... QTY ....

PRICE .... DEPOSIT PAID .... BALANCE PAID ....

PATTERN USED ....

SUPPLIES NEEDED ....

SKETCH / PHOTO

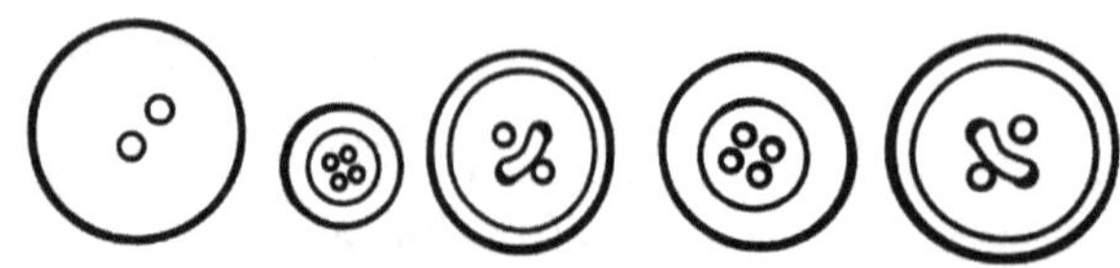

NOTES

Sewing Log Book

DETAILS

PROJECT ....

CREATED FOR ....

DATE STARTED .... DATE COMPLETED ....

ITEM .... QTY ....

PRICE .... DEPOSIT PAID .... BALANCE PAID ....

PATTERN USED ....

SUPPLIES NEEDED ....

SKETCH / PHOTO

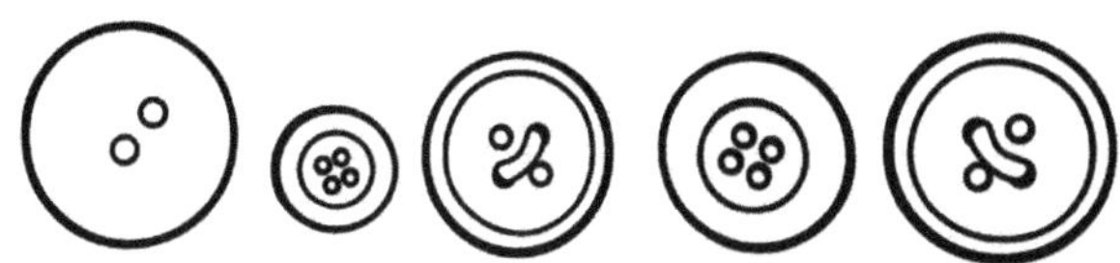

NOTES

....
....
....
....
....
....
....

Sewing Log Book

DETAILS

PROJECT ....

CREATED FOR ....

DATE STARTED .... DATE COMPLETED ....

ITEM .... QTY ....

PRICE .... DEPOSIT PAID .... BALANCE PAID ....

PATTERN USED ....

SUPPLIES NEEDED ....

SKETCH / PHOTO

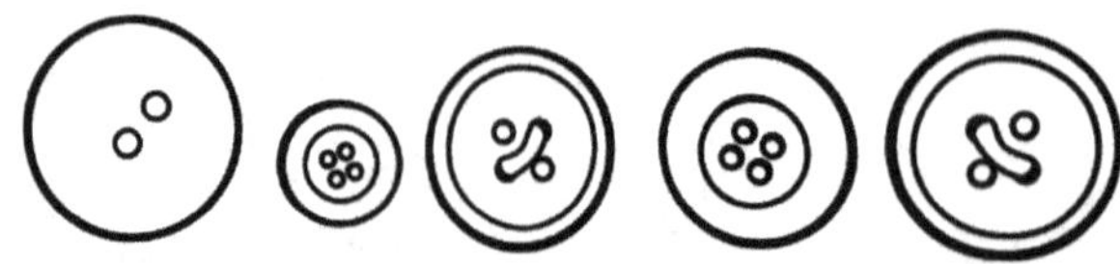

NOTES

....

....

....

....

....

....

Sewing Log Book

DETAILS

PROJECT ....

CREATED FOR ....

DATE STARTED .... DATE COMPLETED ....

ITEM .... QTY ....

PRICE .... DEPOSIT PAID .... BALANCE PAID ....

PATTERN USED ....

SUPPLIES NEEDED ....

SKETCH / PHOTO

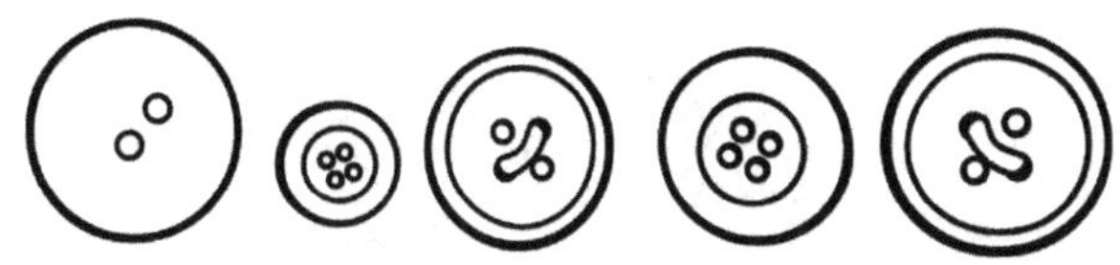

NOTES

....
....
....
....
....
....
....

Sewing Log Book

PROJECT ....

CREATED FOR ....

DATE STARTED .... **DATE COMPLETED** ....

ITEM .... **QTY** ....

PRICE .... **DEPOSIT PAID** .... **BALANCE PAID** ....

PATTERN USED ....

SUPPLIES NEEDED ....

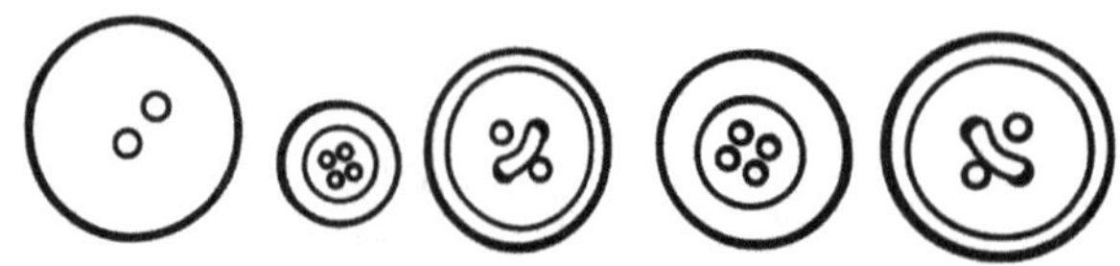

....
....
....
....
....
....
....
....

Sewing Log Book

PROJECT ....

CREATED FOR ....

DATE STARTED .... DATE COMPLETED ....

ITEM .... QTY ....

PRICE .... DEPOSIT PAID .... BALANCE PAID ....

PATTERN USED ....

SUPPLIES NEEDED ....

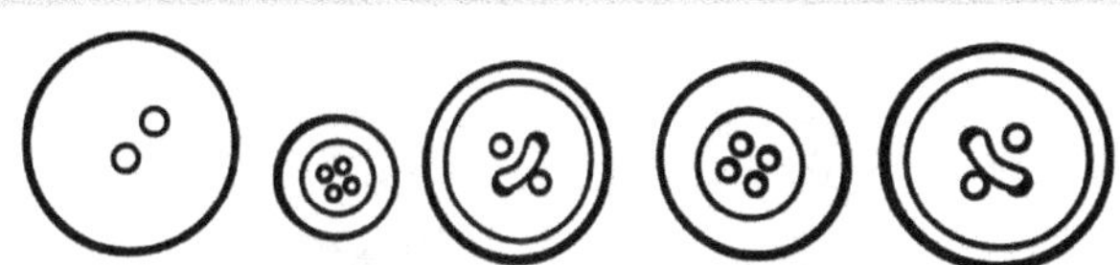

....
....
....
....
....
....
....

Sewing Log Book

DETAILS

PROJECT ....

CREATED FOR ....

DATE STARTED .... **DATE COMPLETED** ....

ITEM .... **QTY** ....

PRICE .... **DEPOSIT PAID** .... **BALANCE PAID** ....

PATTERN USED ....

SUPPLIES NEEDED ....

SKETCH / PHOTO

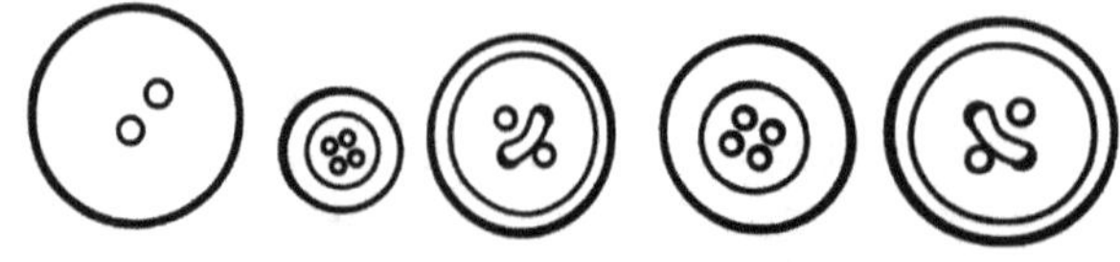

NOTES

....
....
....
....
....
....
....

Sewing Log Book

DETAILS

PROJECT ....

CREATED FOR ....

DATE STARTED .... **DATE COMPLETED** ....

ITEM .... **QTY** ....

PRICE .... **DEPOSIT PAID** .... **BALANCE PAID** ....

PATTERN USED ....

SUPPLIES NEEDED ....

SKETCH / PHOTO

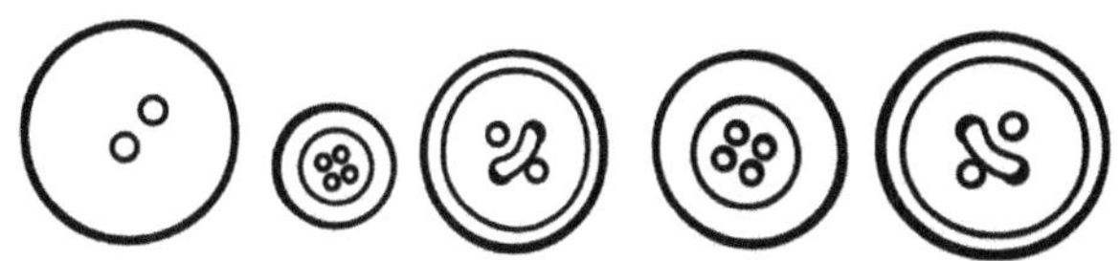

NOTES

....
....
....
....
....
....

Sewing Log Book

DETAILS

PROJECT ....

CREATED FOR ....

DATE STARTED .... DATE COMPLETED ....

ITEM .... QTY ....

PRICE .... DEPOSIT PAID .... BALANCE PAID ....

PATTERN USED ....

SUPPLIES NEEDED ....

SKETCH / PHOTO

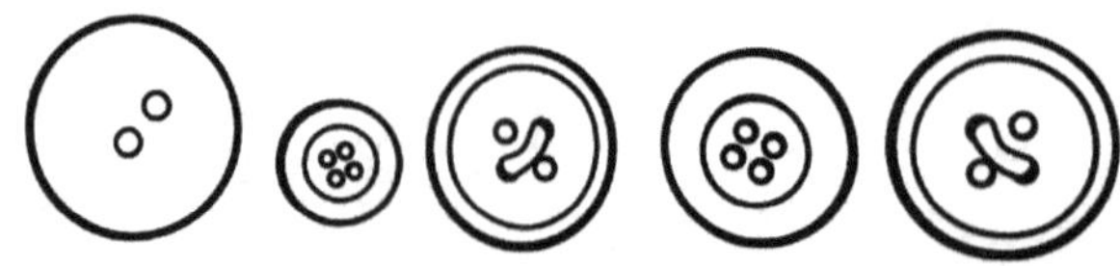

NOTES

....
....
....
....
....
....

Sewing Log Book

DETAILS

PROJECT ....

CREATED FOR ....

DATE STARTED .... **DATE COMPLETED** ....

ITEM .... **QTY** ....

PRICE .... **DEPOSIT PAID** .... **BALANCE PAID** ....

PATTERN USED ....

SUPPLIES NEEDED ....

SKETCH / PHOTO

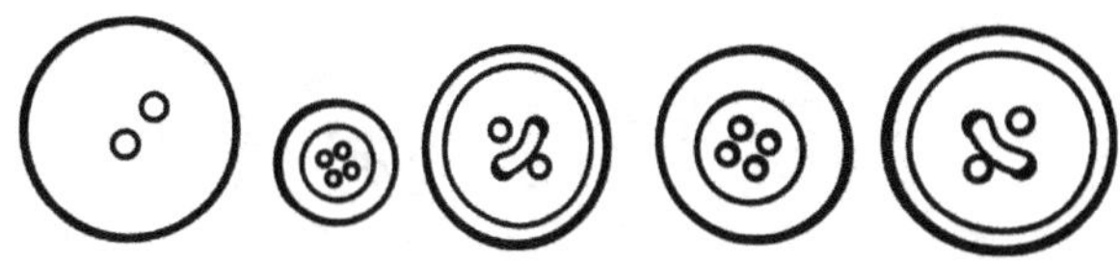

NOTES

....

....

....

....

....

....

....

Sewing Log Book

PROJECT ....

CREATED FOR ....

DATE STARTED .... DATE COMPLETED ....

ITEM .... QTY ....

PRICE .... DEPOSIT PAID .... BALANCE PAID ....

PATTERN USED ....

SUPPLIES NEEDED ....

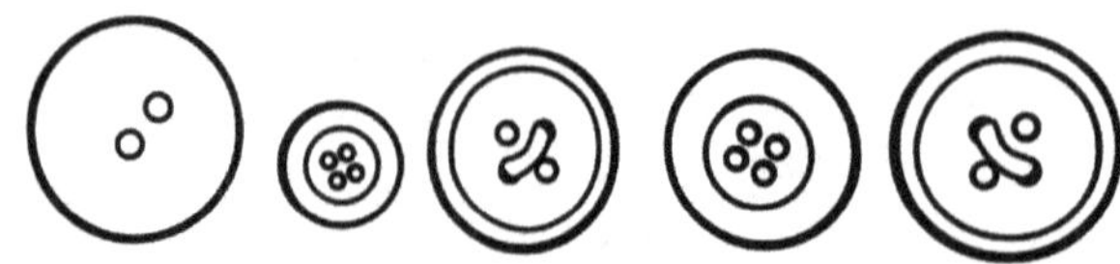

....
....
....
....
....
....
....

Sewing Log Book

DETAILS

PROJECT ....

CREATED FOR ....

DATE STARTED .... DATE COMPLETED ....

ITEM .... QTY ....

PRICE .... DEPOSIT PAID .... BALANCE PAID ....

PATTERN USED ....

SUPPLIES NEEDED ....

SKETCH / PHOTO

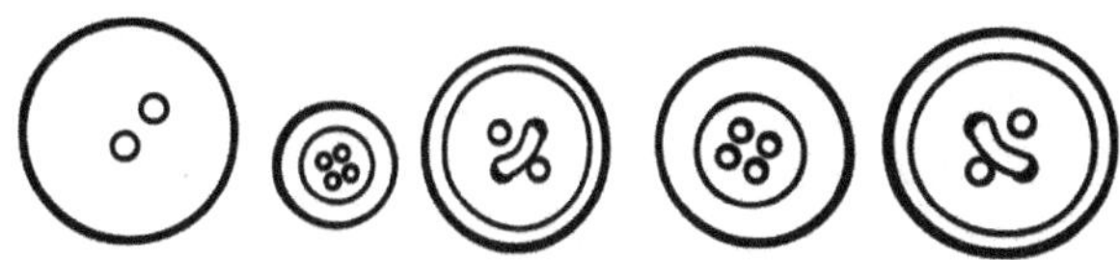

NOTES

....
....
....
....
....
....

Sewing Log Book

DETAILS

PROJECT ....

CREATED FOR ....

DATE STARTED .... DATE COMPLETED ....

ITEM .... QTY ....

PRICE .... DEPOSIT PAID .... BALANCE PAID ....

PATTERN USED ....

SUPPLIES NEEDED ....

SKETCH / PHOTO

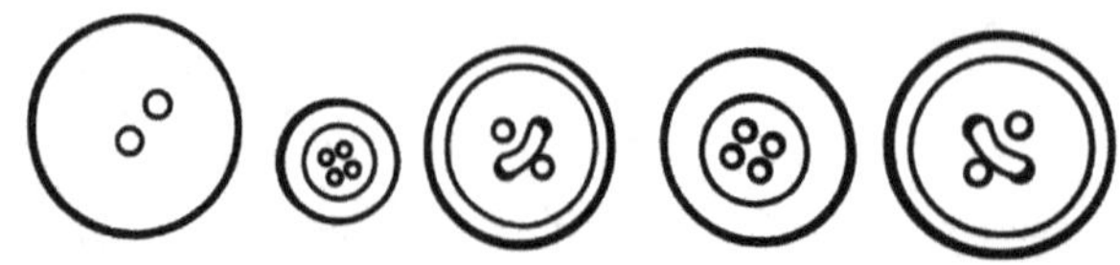

NOTES

....
....
....
....
....
....
....

Sewing Log Book

DETAILS

PROJECT ....

CREATED FOR ....

DATE STARTED .... DATE COMPLETED ....

ITEM .... QTY ....

PRICE .... DEPOSIT PAID .... BALANCE PAID ....

PATTERN USED ....

SUPPLIES NEEDED ....

SKETCH / PHOTO

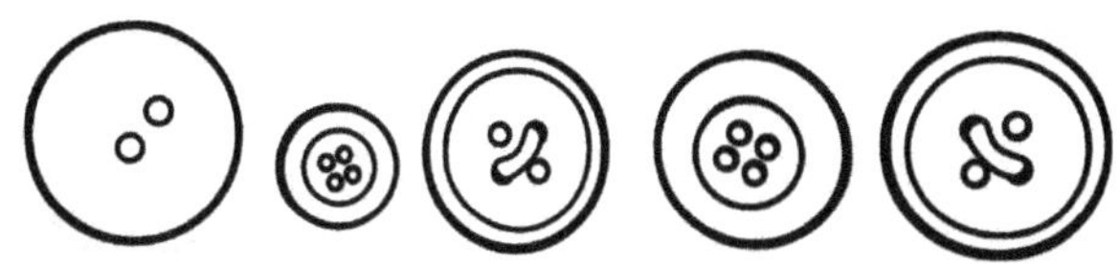

NOTES

....
....
....
....
....
....
....

Sewing Log Book

DETAILS

PROJECT ....

CREATED FOR ....

DATE STARTED .... **DATE COMPLETED** ....

ITEM .... **QTY** ....

PRICE .... **DEPOSIT PAID** .... **BALANCE PAID** ....

PATTERN USED ....

SUPPLIES NEEDED ....

SKETCH / PHOTO

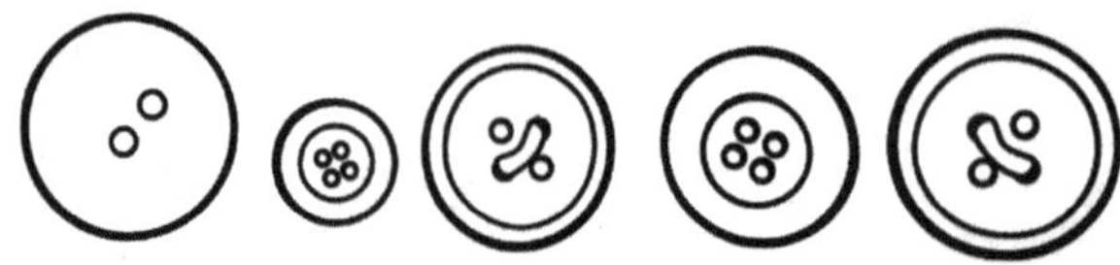

NOTES

....
....
....
....
....
....
....

Sewing Log Book

DETAILS

PROJECT ....

CREATED FOR ....

DATE STARTED .... **DATE COMPLETED** ....

ITEM .... **QTY** ....

PRICE .... **DEPOSIT PAID** .... **BALANCE PAID** ....

PATTERN USED ....

SUPPLIES NEEDED ....

SKETCH / PHOTO

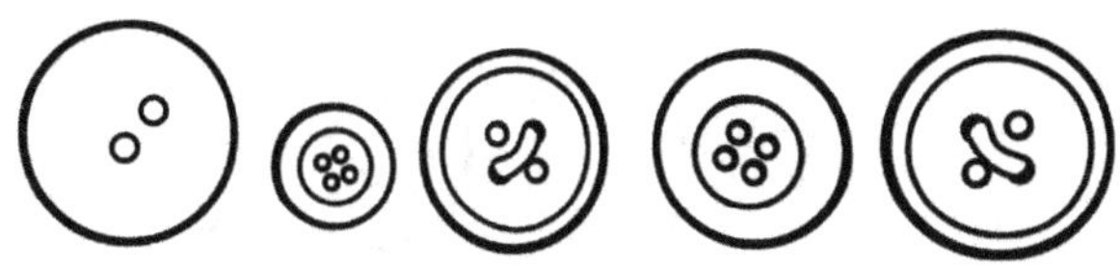

NOTES

....

....

....

....

....

....

....

Sewing Log Book

PROJECT ....

CREATED FOR ....

DATE STARTED .... **DATE COMPLETED** ....

ITEM .... **QTY** ....

PRICE .... **DEPOSIT PAID** .... **BALANCE PAID** ....

PATTERN USED ....

SUPPLIES NEEDED ....

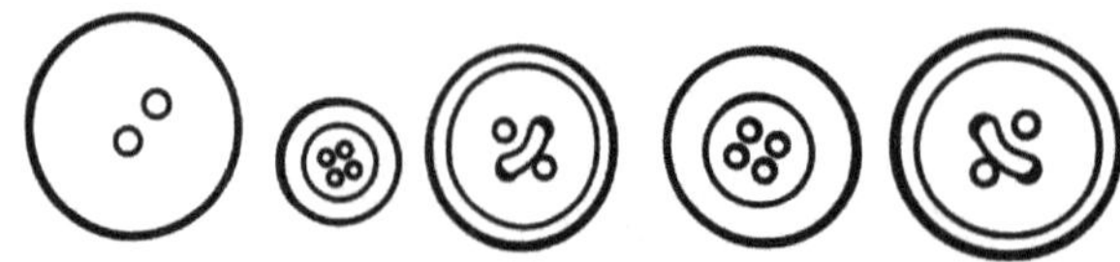

Sewing Log Book

DETAILS

PROJECT ....

CREATED FOR ....

DATE STARTED .... **DATE COMPLETED** ....

ITEM .... **QTY** ....

PRICE .... **DEPOSIT PAID** .... **BALANCE PAID** ....

PATTERN USED ....

SUPPLIES NEEDED ....

SKETCH / PHOTO

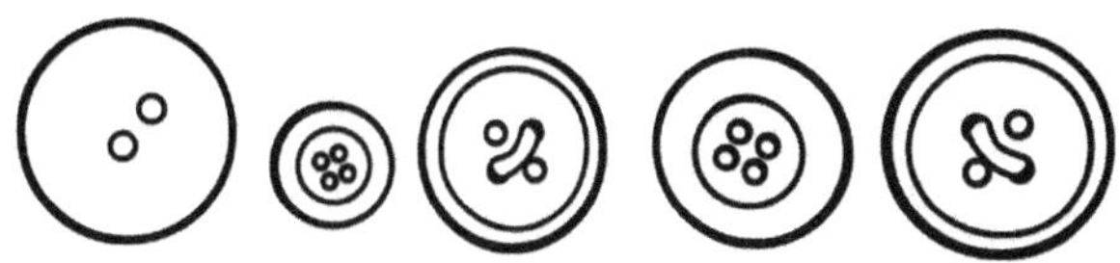

NOTES

....
....
....
....
....
....
....

Sewing Log Book

PROJECT ....

CREATED FOR ....

DATE STARTED .... **DATE COMPLETED** ....

ITEM .... **QTY** ....

PRICE .... **DEPOSIT PAID** .... **BALANCE PAID** ....

PATTERN USED ....

SUPPLIES NEEDED ....

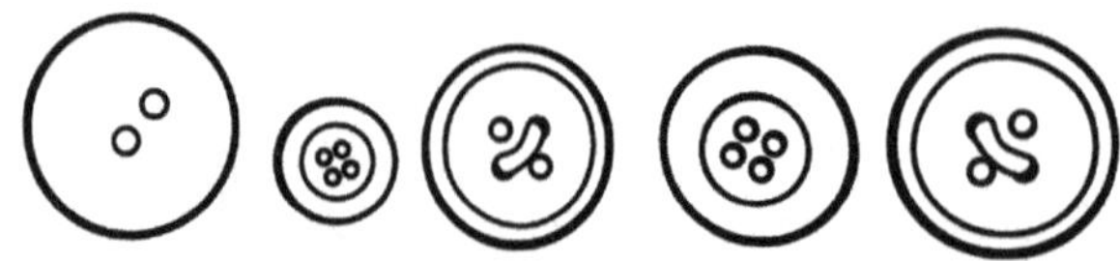

....
....
....
....
....
....
....

Sewing Log Book

PROJECT ....

CREATED FOR ....

DATE STARTED .... **DATE COMPLETED** ....

ITEM .... **QTY** ....

PRICE .... **DEPOSIT PAID** .... **BALANCE PAID** ....

PATTERN USED ....

SUPPLIES NEEDED ....

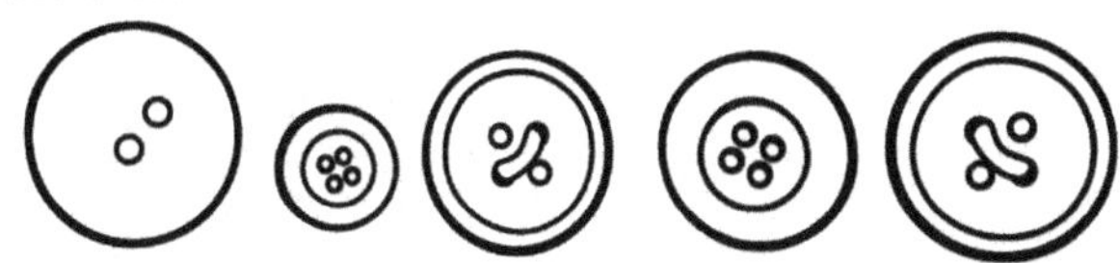

....
....
....
....
....
....

Sewing Log Book

DETAILS

PROJECT ....

CREATED FOR ....

DATE STARTED .... **DATE COMPLETED** ....

ITEM .... **QTY** ....

PRICE .... **DEPOSIT PAID** .... **BALANCE PAID** ....

PATTERN USED ....

SUPPLIES NEEDED ....

SKETCH / PHOTO

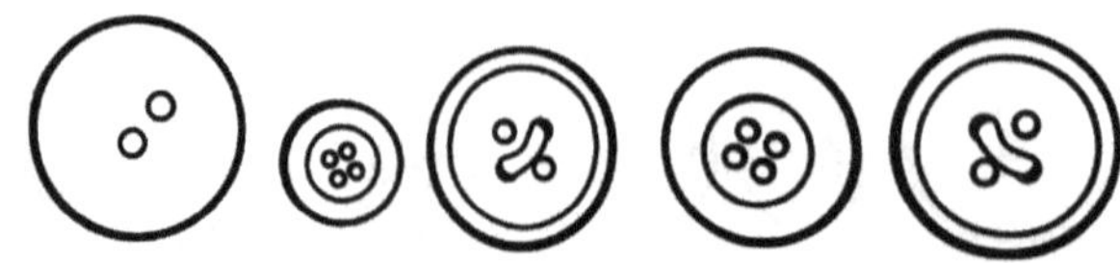

NOTES

....
....
....
....
....
....
....
....

Sewing Log Book

DETAILS

PROJECT ....

CREATED FOR ....

DATE STARTED .... DATE COMPLETED ....

ITEM .... QTY ....

PRICE .... DEPOSIT PAID .... BALANCE PAID ....

PATTERN USED ....

SUPPLIES NEEDED ....

SKETCH / PHOTO

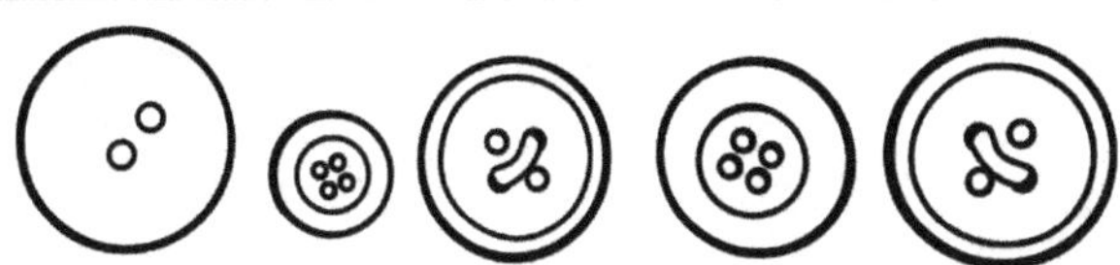

NOTES

....
....
....
....
....
....
....
....

Sewing Log Book

DETAILS

PROJECT ....

CREATED FOR ....

DATE STARTED .... DATE COMPLETED ....

ITEM .... QTY ....

PRICE .... DEPOSIT PAID .... BALANCE PAID ....

PATTERN USED ....

SUPPLIES NEEDED ....

SKETCH / PHOTO

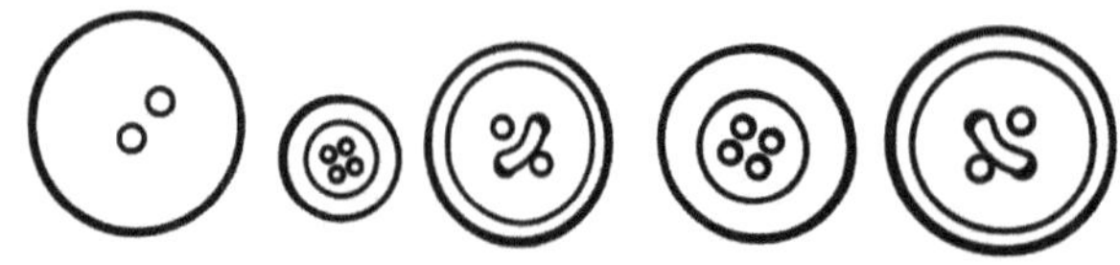

NOTES

....

....

....

....

....

....

....

Sewing Log Book

DETAILS

PROJECT ....

CREATED FOR ....

DATE STARTED .... DATE COMPLETED ....

ITEM .... QTY ....

PRICE .... DEPOSIT PAID .... BALANCE PAID ....

PATTERN USED ....

SUPPLIES NEEDED ....

SKETCH / PHOTO

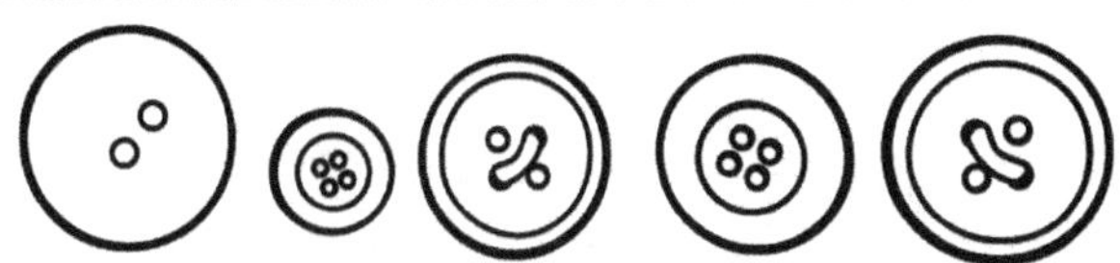

NOTES

....

....

....

....

....

....

....

Sewing Log Book

PROJECT ....

CREATED FOR ....

DATE STARTED .... **DATE COMPLETED** ....

ITEM .... **QTY** ....

PRICE .... **DEPOSIT PAID** .... **BALANCE PAID** ....

PATTERN USED ....

SUPPLIES NEEDED ....

SKETCH / PHOTO

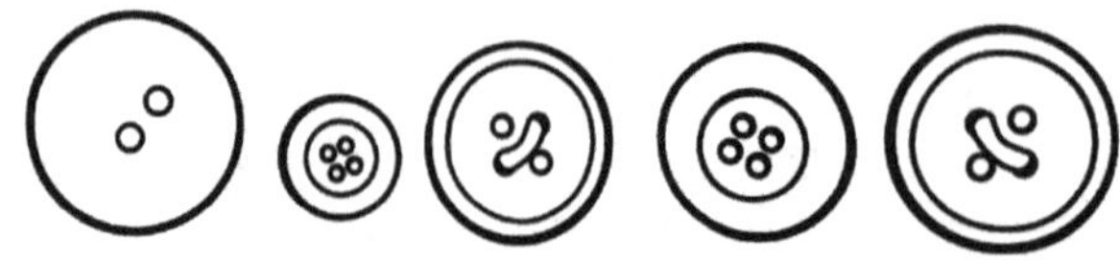

NOTES

....
....
....
....
....
....
....

Sewing Log Book

DETAILS

PROJECT ....

CREATED FOR ....

DATE STARTED .... DATE COMPLETED ....

ITEM .... QTY ....

PRICE .... DEPOSIT PAID .... BALANCE PAID ....

PATTERN USED ....

SUPPLIES NEEDED ....

SKETCH / PHOTO

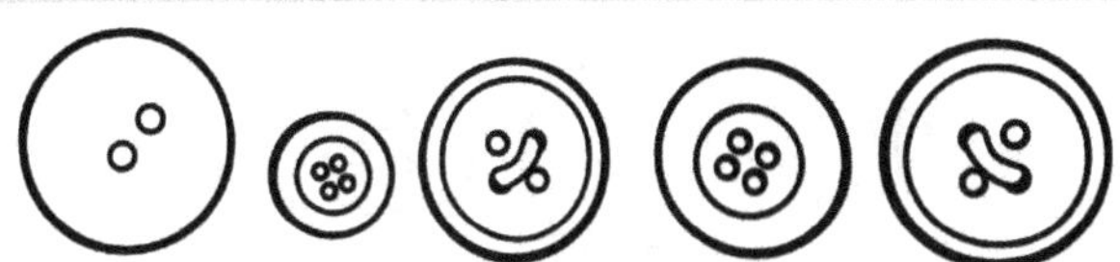

NOTES

....
....
....
....
....
....
....

Sewing Log Book

PROJECT ....

CREATED FOR ....

DATE STARTED .... DATE COMPLETED ....

ITEM .... QTY ....

PRICE .... DEPOSIT PAID .... BALANCE PAID ....

PATTERN USED ....

SUPPLIES NEEDED ....

SKETCH / PHOTO

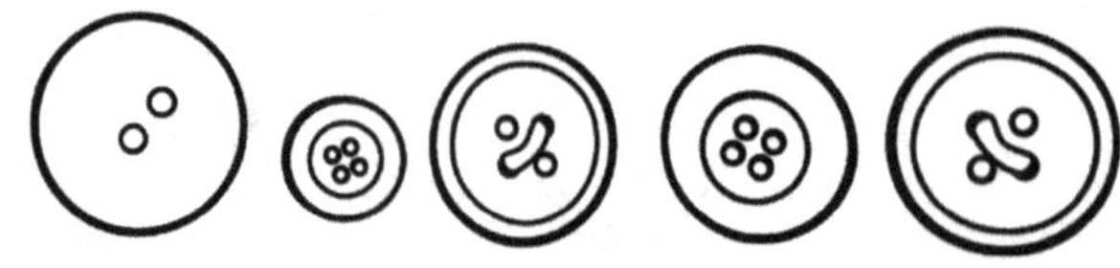

NOTES

....

....

....

....

....

....

....

Sewing Log Book

DETAILS

PROJECT ....

CREATED FOR ....

DATE STARTED .... DATE COMPLETED ....

ITEM .... QTY ....

PRICE .... DEPOSIT PAID .... BALANCE PAID ....

PATTERN USED ....

SUPPLIES NEEDED ....

SKETCH / PHOTO

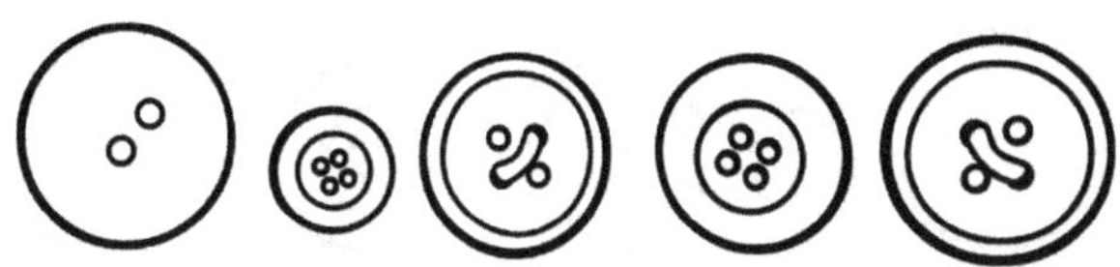

NOTES

....
....
....
....
....
....
....

Sewing Log Book

PROJECT ....

CREATED FOR ....

DATE STARTED .... DATE COMPLETED ....

ITEM .... QTY ....

PRICE .... DEPOSIT PAID .... BALANCE PAID ....

PATTERN USED ....

SUPPLIES NEEDED ....

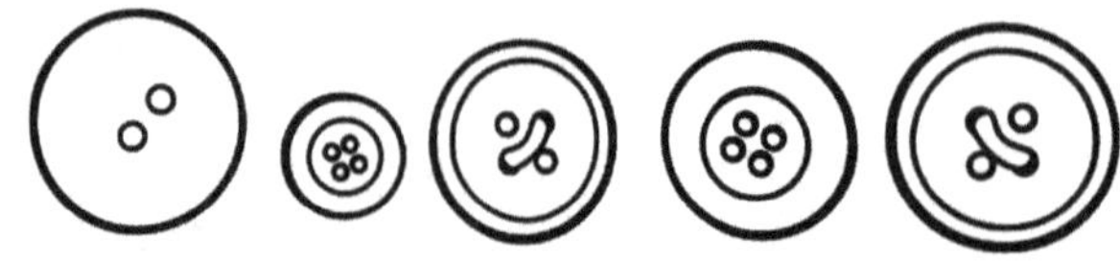

....
....
....
....
....
....
....

Sewing Log Book

PROJECT ....

CREATED FOR ....

DATE STARTED .... DATE COMPLETED ....

ITEM .... QTY ....

PRICE .... DEPOSIT PAID .... BALANCE PAID ....

PATTERN USED ....

SUPPLIES NEEDED ....

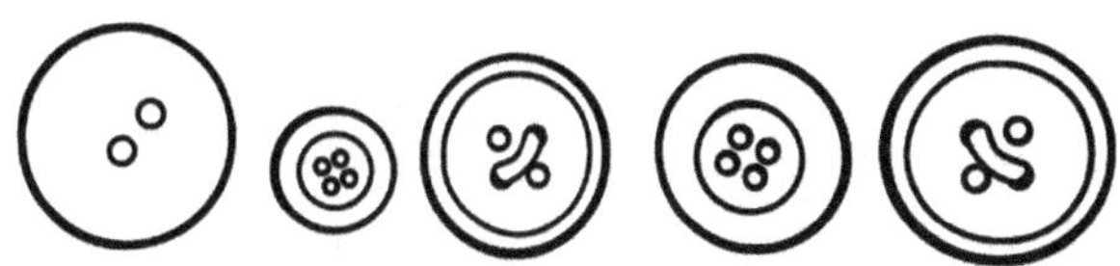

....
....
....
....
....
....
....

Sewing Log Book

DETAILS

PROJECT ....

CREATED FOR ....

DATE STARTED .... DATE COMPLETED ....

ITEM .... QTY ....

PRICE .... DEPOSIT PAID .... BALANCE PAID ....

PATTERN USED ....

SUPPLIES NEEDED ....

SKETCH / PHOTO

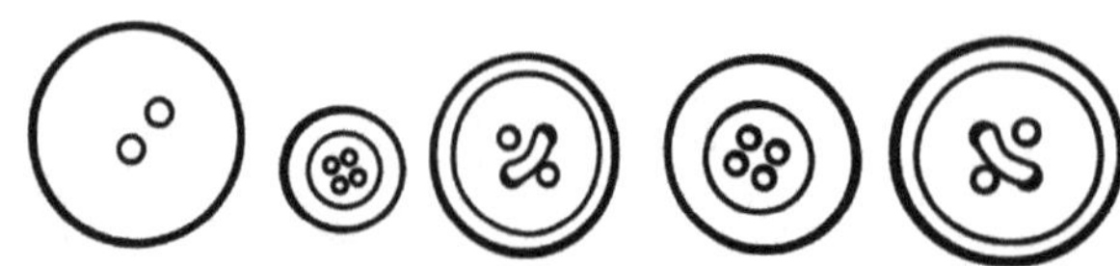

NOTES

....
....
....
....
....
....

Sewing Log Book

DETAILS

PROJECT ....

CREATED FOR ....

DATE STARTED .... **DATE COMPLETED** ....

ITEM .... **QTY** ....

PRICE .... **DEPOSIT PAID** .... **BALANCE PAID** ....

PATTERN USED ....

SUPPLIES NEEDED ....

SKETCH / PHOTO

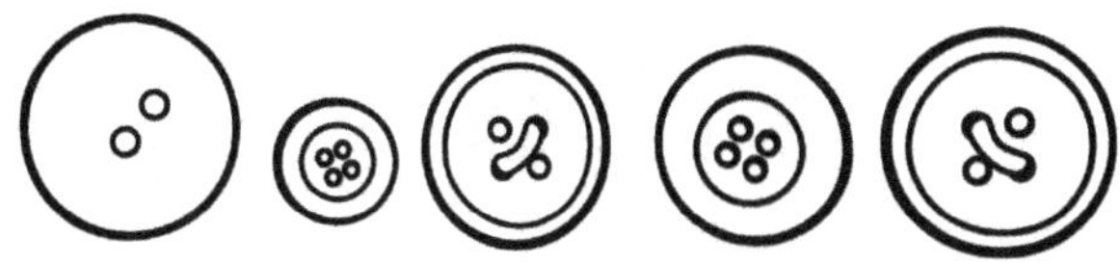

NOTES

....
....
....
....
....
....
....

Sewing Log Book

DETAILS

PROJECT ....

CREATED FOR ....

DATE STARTED .... DATE COMPLETED ....

ITEM .... QTY ....

PRICE .... DEPOSIT PAID .... BALANCE PAID ....

PATTERN USED ....

SUPPLIES NEEDED ....

SKETCH / PHOTO

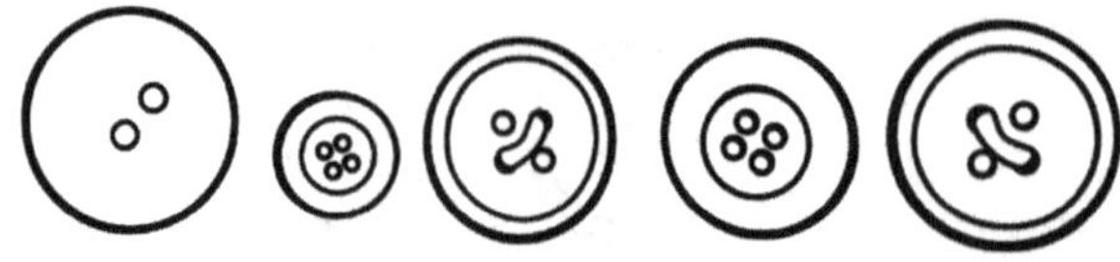

NOTES

....
....
....
....
....
....
....

Sewing Log Book

DETAILS

PROJECT ....

CREATED FOR ....

DATE STARTED .... DATE COMPLETED ....

ITEM .... QTY ....

PRICE .... DEPOSIT PAID .... BALANCE PAID ....

PATTERN USED ....

SUPPLIES NEEDED ....

SKETCH / PHOTO

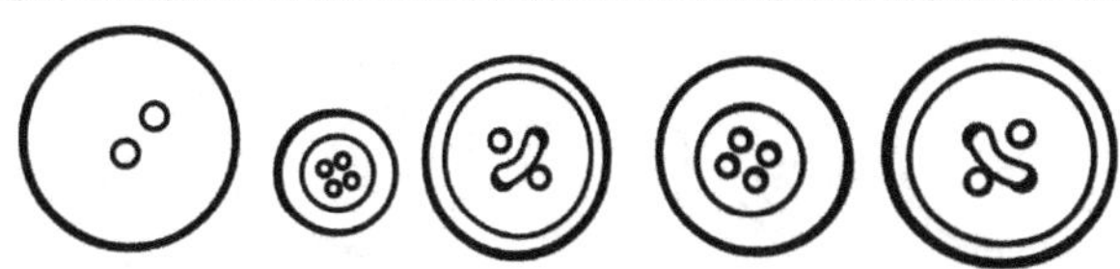

NOTES

....
....
....
....
....
....
....

Sewing Log Book

DETAILS

PROJECT ....

CREATED FOR ....

DATE STARTED .... DATE COMPLETED ....

ITEM .... QTY ....

PRICE .... DEPOSIT PAID .... BALANCE PAID ....

PATTERN USED ....

SUPPLIES NEEDED ....

SKETCH / PHOTO

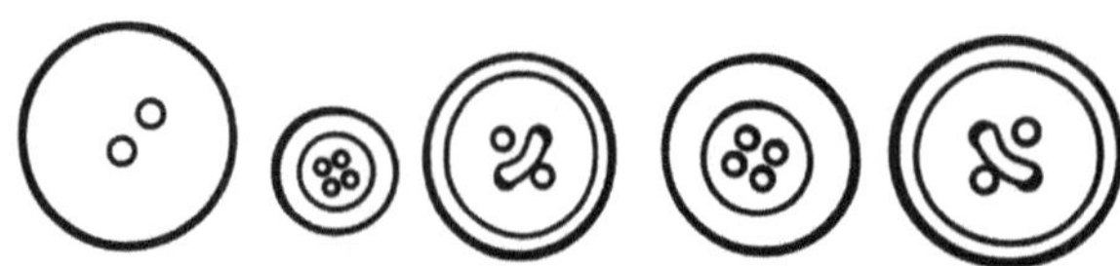

NOTES

....

....

....

....

....

....

....

....

Sewing Log Book

DETAILS

PROJECT ....

CREATED FOR ....

DATE STARTED .... **DATE COMPLETED** ....

ITEM .... **QTY** ....

PRICE .... **DEPOSIT PAID** .... **BALANCE PAID** ....

PATTERN USED ....

SUPPLIES NEEDED ....

SKETCH / PHOTO

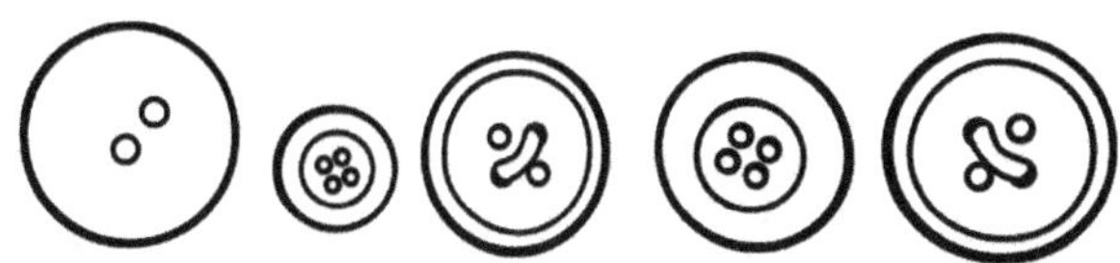

NOTES

....

....

....

....

....

....

....

....

Sewing Log Book

DETAILS

PROJECT ....

CREATED FOR ....

DATE STARTED .... DATE COMPLETED ....

ITEM .... QTY ....

PRICE .... DEPOSIT PAID .... BALANCE PAID ....

PATTERN USED ....

SUPPLIES NEEDED ....

SKETCH / PHOTO

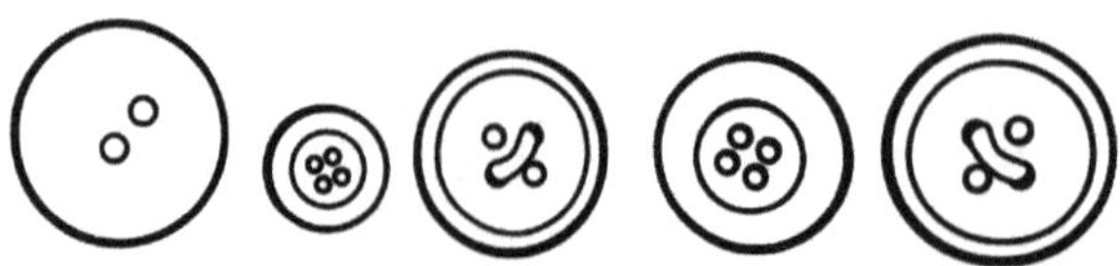

NOTES

....
....
....
....
....
....

Sewing Log Book

DETAILS

PROJECT ....

CREATED FOR ....

DATE STARTED .... **DATE COMPLETED** ....

ITEM .... **QTY** ....

PRICE .... **DEPOSIT PAID** .... **BALANCE PAID** ....

PATTERN USED ....

SUPPLIES NEEDED ....

SKETCH / PHOTO

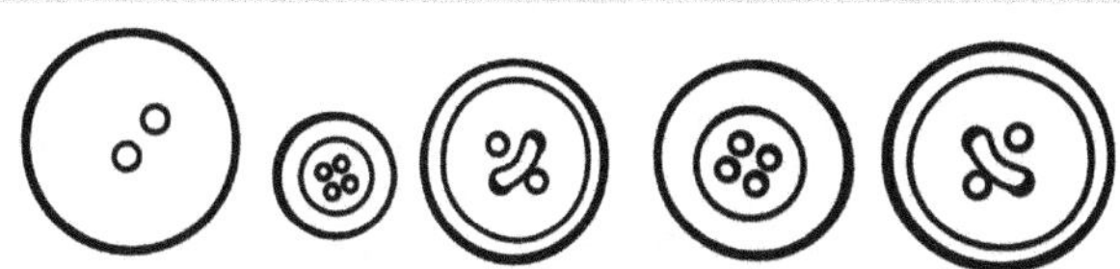

NOTES

....

....

....

....

....

....

Sewing Log Book

DETAILS

PROJECT ....

CREATED FOR ....

DATE STARTED .... DATE COMPLETED ....

ITEM .... QTY ....

PRICE .... DEPOSIT PAID .... BALANCE PAID ....

PATTERN USED ....

SUPPLIES NEEDED ....

SKETCH / PHOTO

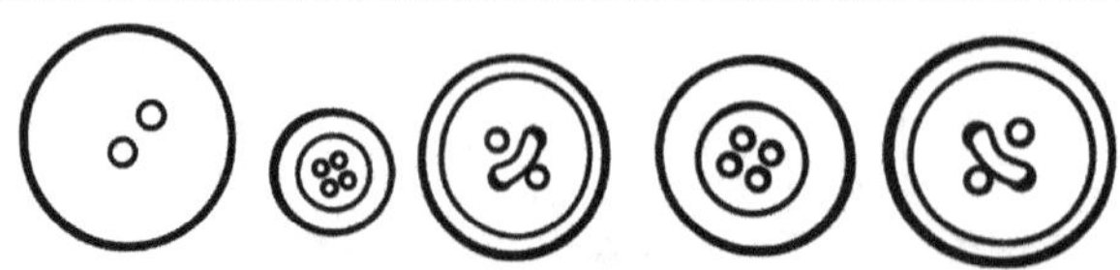

NOTES

....
....
....
....
....
....
....

Sewing Log Book

DETAILS

PROJECT ....

CREATED FOR ....

DATE STARTED .... **DATE COMPLETED** ....

ITEM .... **QTY** ....

PRICE .... **DEPOSIT PAID** .... **BALANCE PAID** ....

PATTERN USED ....

SUPPLIES NEEDED ....

SKETCH / PHOTO

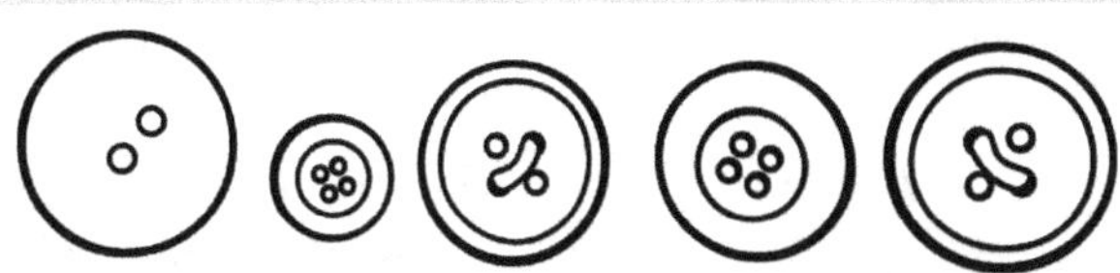

NOTES

....
....
....
....
....
....
....

Sewing Log Book

DETAILS

PROJECT ....

CREATED FOR ....

DATE STARTED .... DATE COMPLETED ....

ITEM .... QTY ....

PRICE .... DEPOSIT PAID .... BALANCE PAID ....

PATTERN USED ....

SUPPLIES NEEDED ....

SKETCH / PHOTO

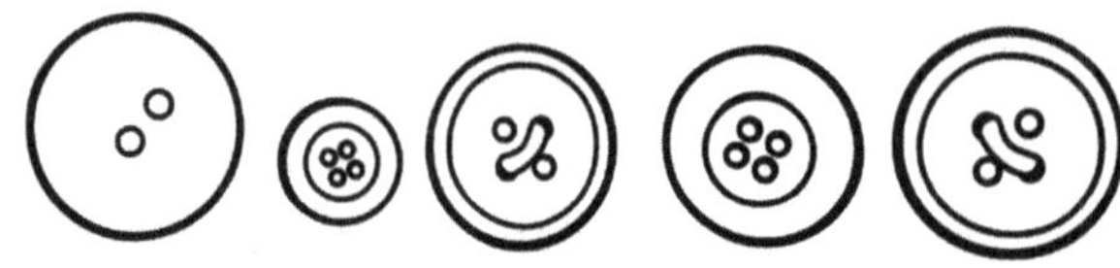

NOTES

Sewing Log Book

DETAILS

PROJECT ....

CREATED FOR ....

DATE STARTED .... DATE COMPLETED ....

ITEM .... QTY ....

PRICE .... DEPOSIT PAID .... BALANCE PAID ....

PATTERN USED ....

SUPPLIES NEEDED ....

SKETCH / PHOTO

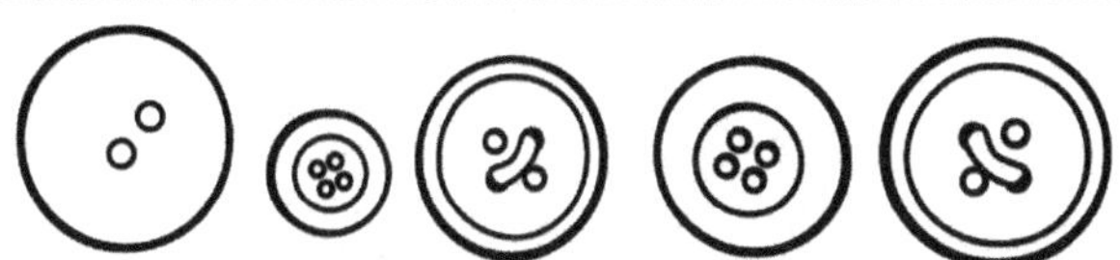

NOTES

....
....
....
....
....
....
....

Sewing Log Book

PROJECT ....

CREATED FOR ....

DATE STARTED .... **DATE COMPLETED** ....

ITEM .... **QTY** ....

PRICE .... **DEPOSIT PAID** .... **BALANCE PAID** ....

PATTERN USED ....

SUPPLIES NEEDED ....

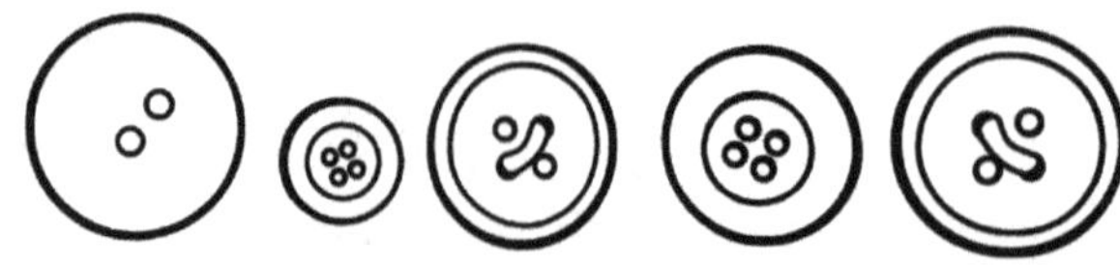

....
....
....
....
....
....
....

Sewing Log Book

PROJECT ....

CREATED FOR ....

DATE STARTED .... **DATE COMPLETED** ....

ITEM .... **QTY** ....

PRICE .... **DEPOSIT PAID** .... **BALANCE PAID** ....

PATTERN USED ....

SUPPLIES NEEDED ....

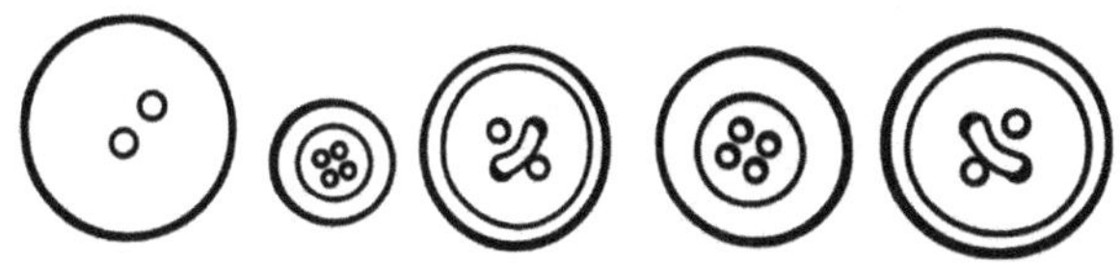

....
....
....
....
....
....
....
....

Sewing Log Book

DETAILS

PROJECT ....

CREATED FOR ....

DATE STARTED .... DATE COMPLETED ....

ITEM .... QTY ....

PRICE .... DEPOSIT PAID .... BALANCE PAID ....

PATTERN USED ....

SUPPLIES NEEDED ....

SKETCH / PHOTO

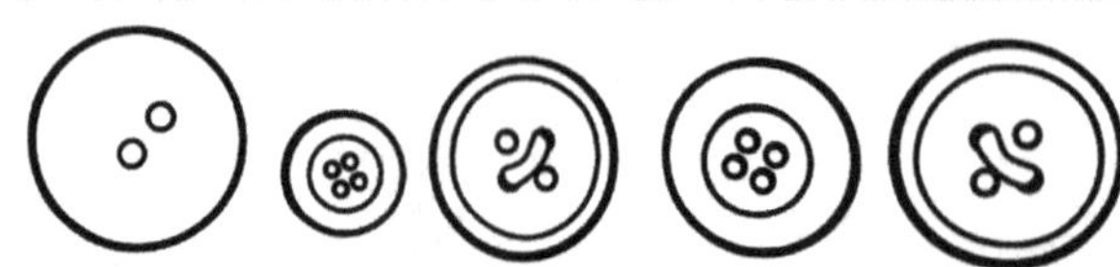

NOTES

....

....

....

....

....

....

....

Sewing Log Book

DETAILS

PROJECT ....

CREATED FOR ....

DATE STARTED .... DATE COMPLETED ....

ITEM .... QTY ....

PRICE .... DEPOSIT PAID .... BALANCE PAID ....

PATTERN USED ....

SUPPLIES NEEDED ....

SKETCH / PHOTO

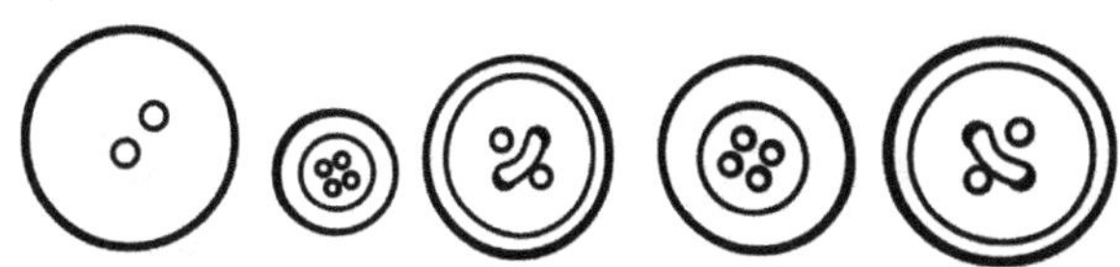

NOTES

....
....
....
....
....
....
....

Sewing Log Book

DETAILS

PROJECT ....

CREATED FOR ....

DATE STARTED .... DATE COMPLETED ....

ITEM .... QTY ....

PRICE .... DEPOSIT PAID .... BALANCE PAID ....

PATTERN USED ....

SUPPLIES NEEDED ....

SKETCH / PHOTO

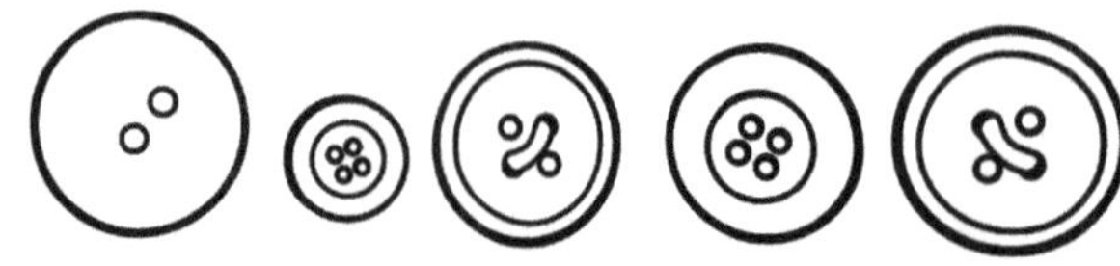

NOTES

....
....
....
....
....
....
....

Sewing Log Book

DETAILS

PROJECT ....

CREATED FOR ....

DATE STARTED .... DATE COMPLETED ....

ITEM .... QTY ....

PRICE .... DEPOSIT PAID .... BALANCE PAID ....

PATTERN USED ....

SUPPLIES NEEDED ....

SKETCH / PHOTO

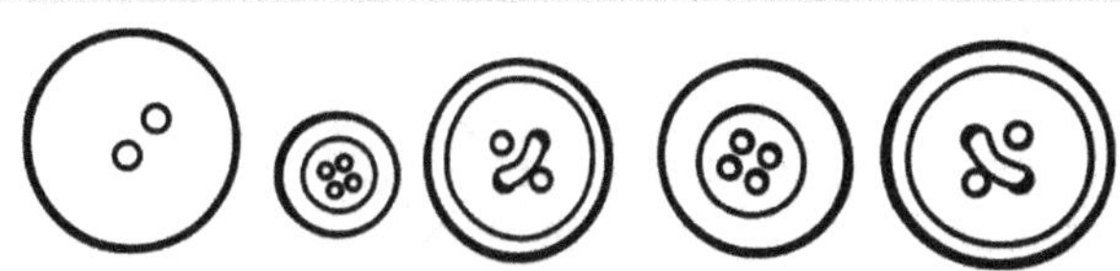

NOTES

....
....
....
....
....
....
....

Sewing Log Book

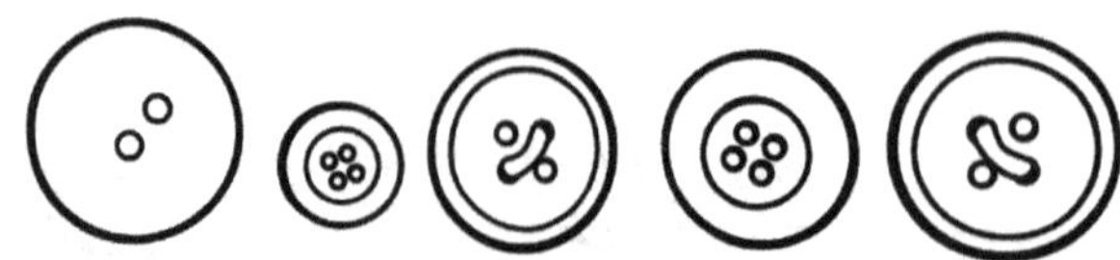

Sewing Log Book

PROJECT ....

CREATED FOR ....

DATE STARTED .... **DATE COMPLETED** ....

ITEM .... **QTY** ....

PRICE .... **DEPOSIT PAID** .... **BALANCE PAID** ....

PATTERN USED ....

SUPPLIES NEEDED ....

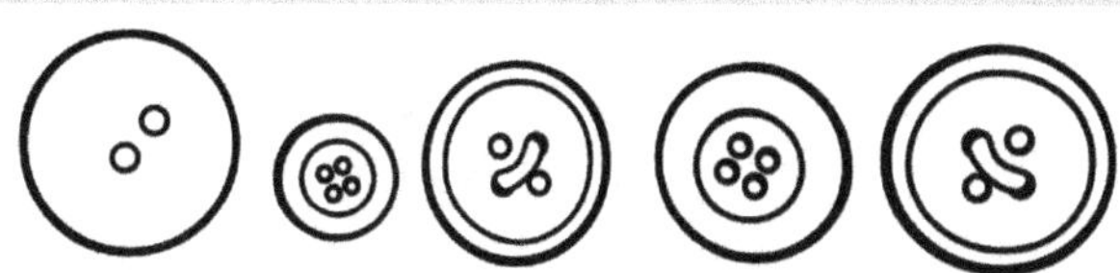

....
....
....
....
....
....

Sewing Log Book

DETAILS

PROJECT ....

CREATED FOR ....

DATE STARTED .... DATE COMPLETED ....

ITEM .... QTY ....

PRICE .... DEPOSIT PAID .... BALANCE PAID ....

PATTERN USED ....

SUPPLIES NEEDED ....

SKETCH / PHOTO

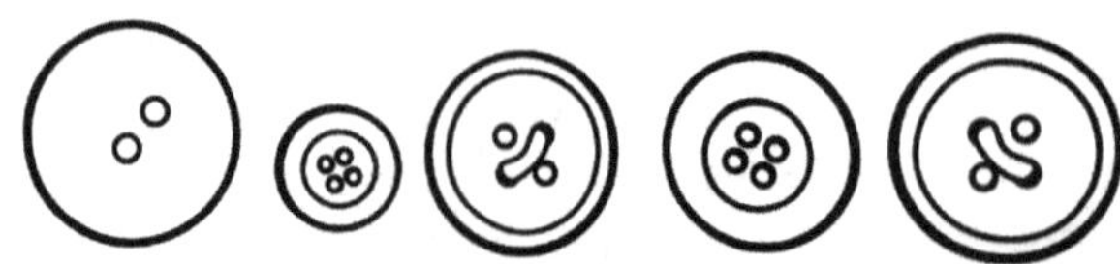

NOTES

....

....

....

....

....

....

....

Sewing Log Book

DETAILS

PROJECT ....

CREATED FOR ....

DATE STARTED .... DATE COMPLETED ....

ITEM .... QTY ....

PRICE .... DEPOSIT PAID .... BALANCE PAID ....

PATTERN USED ....

SUPPLIES NEEDED ....

SKETCH / PHOTO

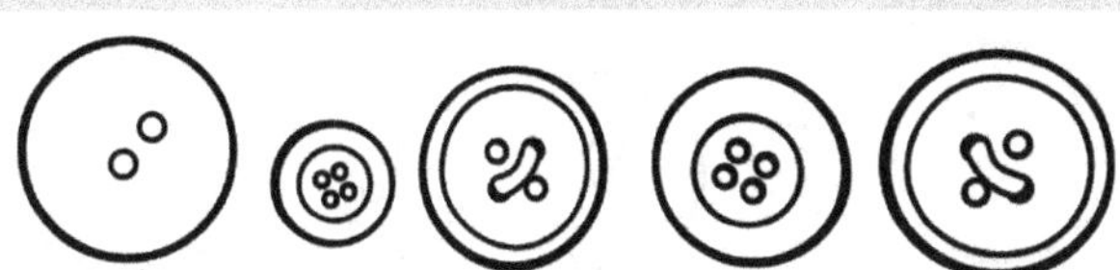

NOTES

....
....
....
....
....
....
....

Sewing Log Book

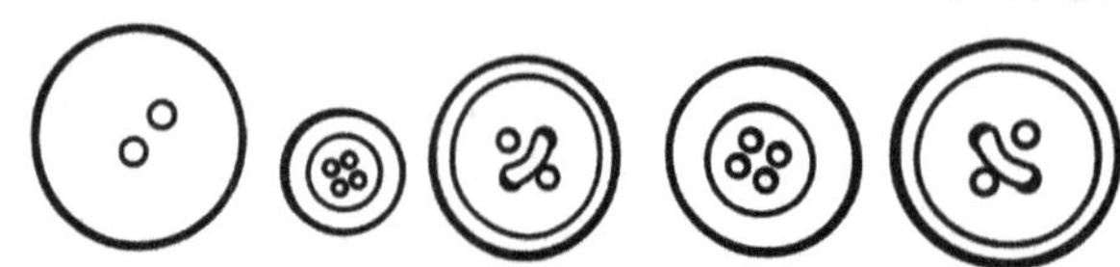

Sewing Log Book

DETAILS

PROJECT ....

CREATED FOR ....

DATE STARTED .... DATE COMPLETED ....

ITEM .... QTY ....

PRICE .... DEPOSIT PAID .... BALANCE PAID ....

PATTERN USED ....

SUPPLIES NEEDED ....

SKETCH / PHOTO

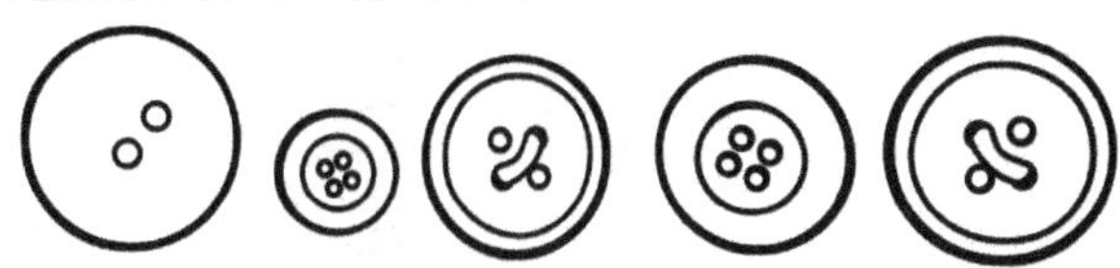

NOTES

....

....

....

....

....

....

....

Sewing Log Book

DETAILS

PROJECT ....

CREATED FOR ....

DATE STARTED .... DATE COMPLETED ....

ITEM .... QTY ....

PRICE .... DEPOSIT PAID .... BALANCE PAID ....

PATTERN USED ....

SUPPLIES NEEDED ....

SKETCH / PHOTO

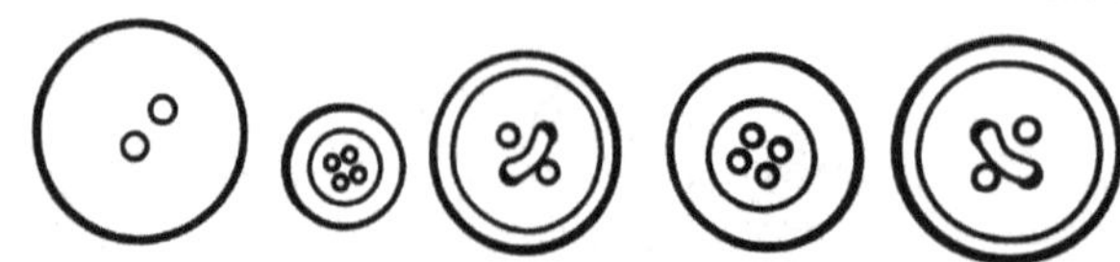

NOTES

....

....

....

....

....

....

....

....

Sewing Log Book

DETAILS

PROJECT ....

CREATED FOR ....

DATE STARTED .... DATE COMPLETED ....

ITEM .... QTY ....

PRICE .... DEPOSIT PAID .... BALANCE PAID ....

PATTERN USED ....

SUPPLIES NEEDED ....

SKETCH / PHOTO

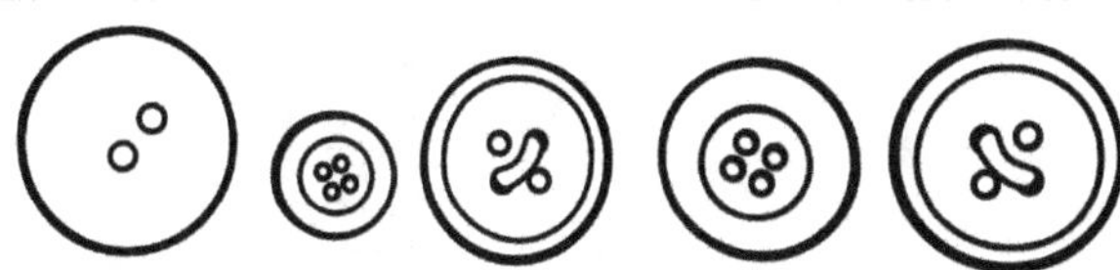

NOTES

....

....

....

....

....

....

....

Sewing Log Book

PROJECT ....

CREATED FOR ....

DATE STARTED .... **DATE COMPLETED** ....

ITEM .... **QTY** ....

PRICE .... **DEPOSIT PAID** .... **BALANCE PAID** ....

PATTERN USED ....

SUPPLIES NEEDED ....

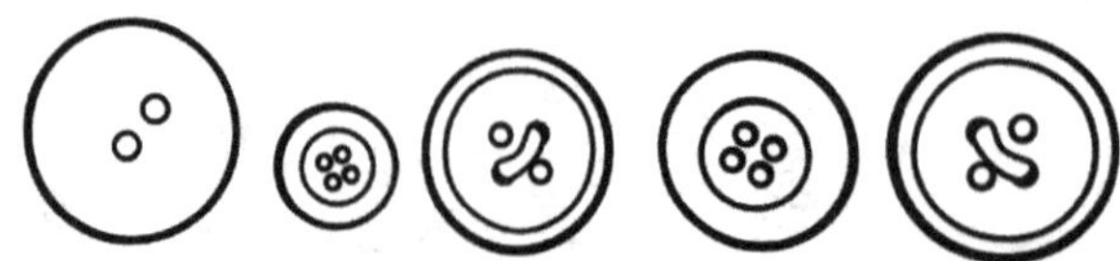

....
....
....
....
....
....
....

Sewing Log Book

DETAILS

PROJECT ....

CREATED FOR ....

DATE STARTED .... **DATE COMPLETED** ....

ITEM .... **QTY** ....

PRICE .... **DEPOSIT PAID** .... **BALANCE PAID** ....

PATTERN USED ....

SUPPLIES NEEDED ....

SKETCH / PHOTO

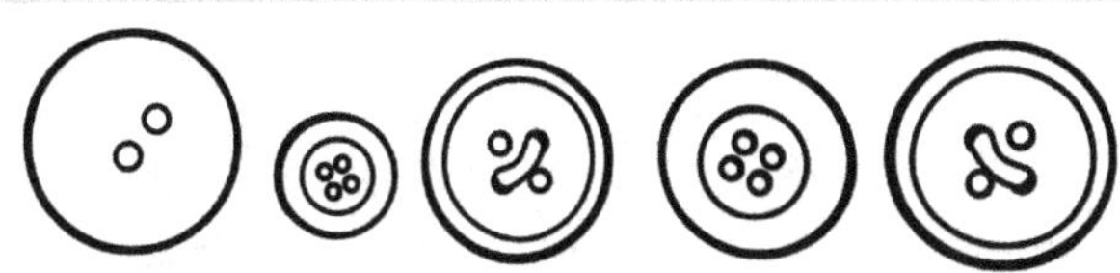

NOTES

....
....
....
....
....
....
....

Sewing Log Book

PROJECT ....

CREATED FOR ....

DATE STARTED .... **DATE COMPLETED** ....

ITEM .... **QTY** ....

PRICE .... **DEPOSIT PAID** .... **BALANCE PAID** ....

PATTERN USED ....

SUPPLIES NEEDED ....

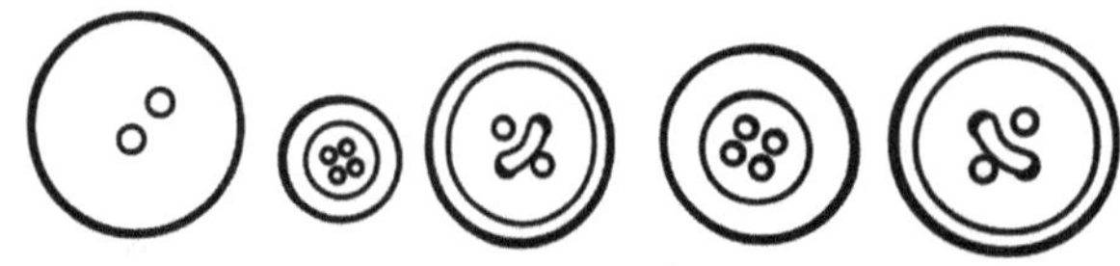

....
....
....
....
....
....
....

Sewing Log Book

DETAILS

PROJECT ....

CREATED FOR ....

DATE STARTED .... DATE COMPLETED ....

ITEM .... QTY ....

PRICE .... DEPOSIT PAID .... BALANCE PAID ....

PATTERN USED ....

SUPPLIES NEEDED ....

SKETCH / PHOTO

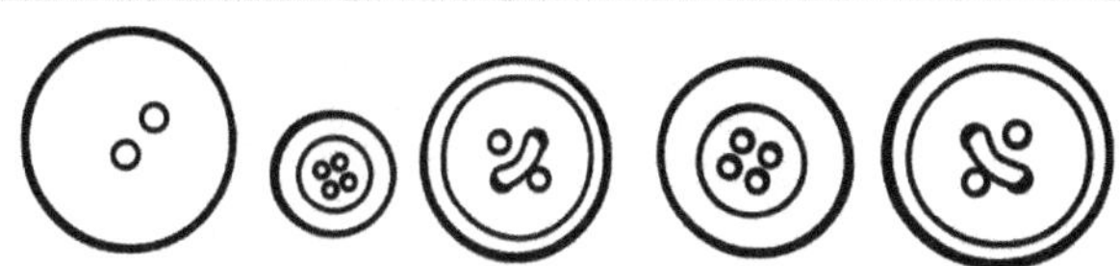

NOTES

....
....
....
....
....
....
....

Sewing Log Book

DETAILS

PROJECT ....

CREATED FOR ....

DATE STARTED .... DATE COMPLETED ....

ITEM .... QTY ....

PRICE .... DEPOSIT PAID .... BALANCE PAID ....

PATTERN USED ....

SUPPLIES NEEDED ....

SKETCH / PHOTO

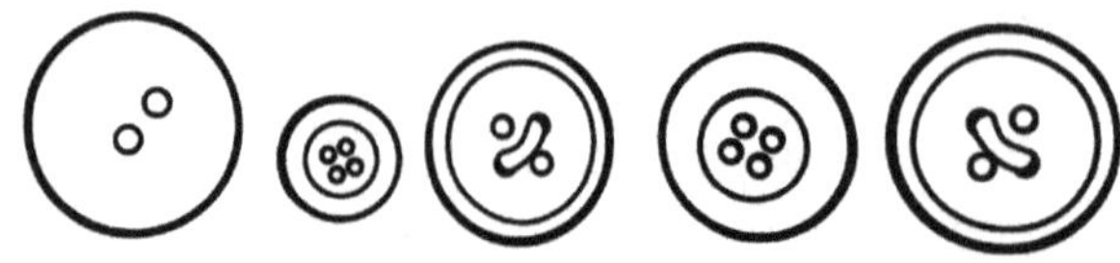

NOTES

....
....
....
....
....
....

Sewing Log Book

DETAILS

PROJECT ....

CREATED FOR ....

DATE STARTED .... **DATE COMPLETED** ....

ITEM .... **QTY** ....

PRICE .... **DEPOSIT PAID** .... **BALANCE PAID** ....

PATTERN USED ....

SUPPLIES NEEDED ....

SKETCH / PHOTO

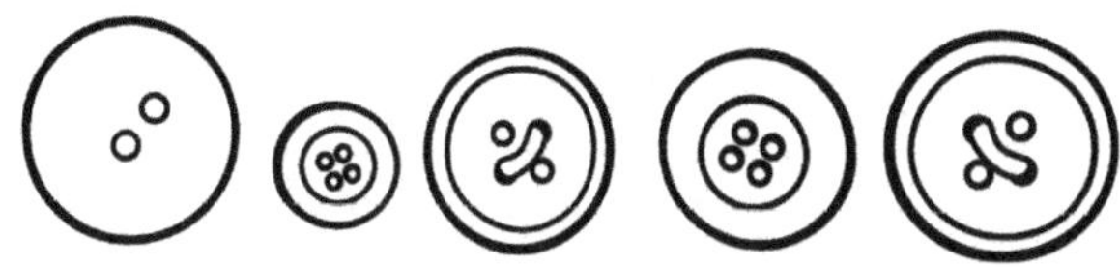

NOTES

....
....
....
....
....
....
....

Sewing Log Book

DETAILS

PROJECT ....

CREATED FOR ....

DATE STARTED .... DATE COMPLETED ....

ITEM .... QTY ....

PRICE .... DEPOSIT PAID .... BALANCE PAID ....

PATTERN USED ....

SUPPLIES NEEDED ....

SKETCH / PHOTO

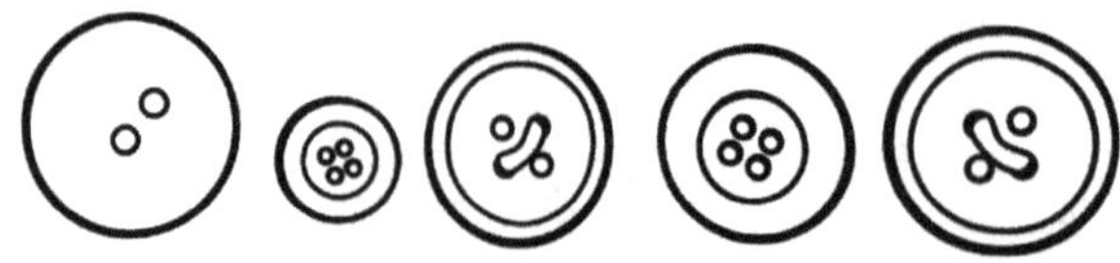

NOTES

....
....
....
....
....
....
....